Life Off Earth

Ian Ridpath

LIFE OFF EARTH

GRANADA
London Toronto Sydney New York

To Gerard O'Neill

Published by Granada Publishing 1983
Granada Publishing Limited
Frogmore, St Albans, Herts AL2 2NF
and
36 Golden Square, London W1R 4AH
515 Madison Avenue, New York, NY 10022, USA
117 York Street, Sydney, NSW 2000, Australia
60 International Blvd, Rexdale, Ontario, R9W 6J2, Canada
61 Beach Road, Auckland, New Zealand

British Library Cataloguing in Publication Data
Ridpath, Ian
   Life off earth.
   1. Life on other planets
   I. Title
   574.999   QB54

ISBN 0 246 11933 0

Printed in Italy by
New Interlitho, Milan

GRANADA ®
GRANADA PUBLISHING ®

Acknowledgements

This book began when I was asked to give the Annual Lecture to the School Natural Science Society in London in 1981. The previous year the Society's president, David Attenborough, had spoken about Life on Earth, the title of his famous TV series; the Society's chairman, Peter Shaw, decided that Life off Earth was the obvious sequel and, knowing my interest in the subject as a science writer, asked me to tackle it. The concept seemed so good that I could not resist expanding it into a book. I must thank Peter Shaw for inviting me to give that initial lecture, and for suggesting the title.

As ever, there would be no book to write were it not for the scientists who endeavour to push back the frontiers of human knowledge. In particular, I wish to thank those who have responded to my requests for specific information for this book: John Billingham of NASA's Ames Research Center; George Gatewood of Allegheny Observatory; Frank Tipler of Tulane University. I should also like to thank Dr Alan Benson of the Royal Air Force Institute of Aviation Medicine, Farnborough, who read and commented on the first three chapters and who let me try out the rotating chair in his laboratory used for research into motion sickness. Needless to say, I am responsible for the final form of the text.

Part of Chapter 5 appeared in slightly different form in New Scientist, 25 March, 1982; and Chapter 10 is based on an address I gave in a debate at the Oxford Union on 28 October, 1981.

One sad piece of news during the preparation of this book was the untimely death of Krzysztof Serkowski, an astronomer of great ingenuity and charm, who was leading the team at the University of Arizona's Lunar and Planetary Laboratory in the hunt for planetary systems of other stars. That work, now under the direction of Robert McMillan, promises to produce the positive results for which Krzysztof had hoped.

On the subject of planetary searches, the Extrasolar Planetary Foundation exists to gather funds to support the search for planetary systems of other stars. Their address is: Observatory Station, Pittsburgh, Pennsylvania 15214, USA. Another private organization devoted to raising funds for the support of space exploration and the search for extraterrestrial intelligence is Delta Vee (president, Stan Kent), 3033 Moorpark Avenue, Suite 27, San Jose, California 95128. The Planetary Society (president, Carl Sagan), has been formed to coordinate popular support for planetary exploration, and is also collecting funds for extraterrestrial life research. Their address is 110 South Euclid Avenue, Pasadena, California 91101, USA.

Readers might also be interested to know of a magazine devoted to the search for life in space called AstroSearch. Its address is PO Box 3294, Saratoga, California 95070, USA.

I.R.

Contents

Introduction

In twos and threes they came, through the quickening gloom of the October evening, crossing the field to the grassed hill as if ascending to the sermon on the mount. We were in the suburbs of north-east London, on the edge of a forest, and we had come to listen to a member of the local group of unidentified flying object (UFO) enthusiasts tell us of a sighting that had occurred not long before near where we stood. The story went like this.

Shortly before 4 AM on May 3, 1977, Police had been called to the scene in a recreation area on the edge of Hainault forest (an outlying part of Epping forest) by a man who telephoned to report a UFO. When the Police arrived there was no sign of the caller, but they noticed a red pulsating light near a lake; as they approached, the light receded into the forest and vanished. Subsequently, a broken bush was found in the vicinity which, we were told, showed signs of having been crushed as though by a force from above. Were we to believe that a glowing alien probe had temporarily nestled in this bush on the outskirts of London, unnoticed by anyone but a startled passer-by? The group of would-be UFO spotters gazed in hushed wonder towards the site of the alleged landing, now lost in darkness.

We huddled closer as photographs were passed around under the light of torches – pictures of saucer-like craft allegedly flitting through the skies above the United States. Certain lucky humans, we were told, had even been aboard some of these craft and had met their occupants. For the UFO group on that grassy hill in Hainault, Essex, the sense of mystery was deepened by these photographs. This was at the time of a wave of UFO sightings in Britain. As we looked up to the sky again, we could sense what each other was thinking. Would any of us experience such an awesome encounter? Might that glowing UFO reappear here in Hainault if we wished hard enough? Our group settled down expectantly under the night sky for a UFO watch. There was a reawakening of that familiar childhood feeling of anticipation as when awaiting the Christmas Eve arrival of Santa Claus.

We saw stars, aircraft, and the occasional satellite. On the distant horizon, a red light flashed on top of the Post Office telecommunication tower in central London, standing guard over the city like a Martian fighting machine from H.G. Wells's War of the Worlds. But of UFOs, still less aliens from another planet, we saw nothing.

Similar scenes are repeated at UFO sky watches throughout the world. There are many theories about UFOs, but the most persistent is that they are visitors from other worlds. Whether or not that is true – and I shall be giving my own views on the whole complex subject in Chapter 10 – there are large numbers of people who would like it to be true. UFO watchers are searching for the reassurance that we are not alone in space, that there is life off Earth – an entirely plausible speculation, but one in which wishful thinking is all too often substituted for hard fact.

Scientists also are searching for evidence of life off Earth. But they are not concentrating on UFOs, a subject which most scientists dismiss. Instead, they are scanning the skies to hear the faint whispers of radio transmissions from other beings. Another approach is to search for evidence of simple life forms on the planets of our own solar system by sending space probes. Now that we have available the techniques of radio communication and space probe exploration we must use them to the full, for the discovery of life off Earth would be one of the most important in history, changing our entire attitudes towards the Universe and to ourselves. Ours is the first generation that instead of merely speculating about life off Earth can actually carry out experiments to test those speculations. As yet there is no confirmation that life off Earth exists. But the chances of success seem sufficiently good, and the reward potentially so great, that it is worth continuing the effort.

Paradoxically, the discovery of life off Earth would tell us a great deal more about life on Earth, for scientists still do not fully understand how life arose on this planet. At the chemical level of the living cell, all life on Earth displays an impressive uniformity which cannot be coincidence. Rather, it suggests that every living thing on Earth is descended from a common ancestor. There have been at least simple organisms on Earth for three-quarters of our planet's 4.6-billion-year history. But is life on Earth a freak, or is it typical of what the Universe has to offer? Until we find examples of life off Earth to compare ourselves with, we cannot know.

In theory, life off Earth ought to be abundant. Our Sun is but one star in a Galaxy of at least 100 billion stars, many of which may be accompanied by planets, and some of those planets could harbour life. Statistically, therefore, life off Earth seems inevitable. That's easy to say, but far more difficult to prove. Scientists are encouraged in their belief that life off Earth is abundant by the fact that the right chemicals for life – compounds based on carbon – are spread plentifully throughout the Galaxy. Radio astronomers can detect them in clouds of matter where new stars – and, we presume, planets – are being born.

Assuming that there is life out there, how could we find out about it? Humans are exceedingly chatty creatures – witness the boom in telephone traffic and citizens' band radio – so it seems reasonable to suppose that alien beings, if they exist, will be equally communicative. The interstellar wavebands could be humming with the transmissions of other creatures – if only we knew how to tune in.

But we must also bear in mind the possibility that civilizations such as our own may be rare or even non-existent in the Galaxy. If civilizations similar to our own have arisen in the past, they may already have wiped themselves out through disasters such as nuclear warfare, overpopulation, famine or pollution. On the other hand, it may be that by some biological and statistical freak we are the first high-tech civilization to arise in the Galaxy –

after all, *someone* has to be first. In either case, there would be no one around for us to exchange radio messages with, and so our listening projects would inevitably be doomed to failure. But even if this gloomy eventuality were true, think of the exotic flora and fauna, and maybe even stone-age cultures, that must exist out there as yet unknown and unseen, to be discovered by the first space-age Columbus from Earth.

We cannot yet send probes to the planets of other stars, because the stars are so far away that present-day rockets would take 100,000 years to reach the nearest. Next century we will, if we choose to do so, be able to build craft powered by the release of nuclear energy, that could reach the nearest stars inside a human lifetime. Such craft would be unmanned probes on a one-way trip. Eventually, expeditions with human crews could follow, to set up colonies around favourable stars, continuing the spread of life that began when the first fish crawled out of the sea onto land.

There is a deep and fundamental link between life and the stars, as revealed by modern astrophysics: the elements heavier than hydrogen and helium – including carbon, nitrogen, oxygen, and other atoms of our bodies – are made by nuclear reactions inside stars. Those atoms are scattered into space when the stars die, to be collected up into new stars and planets. Without stars, there would be no life. In a very real sense, we are all made of starstuff. We are the children of the stars, and what we are now seeing is a return to the stars.

This book looks at life off Earth in all its senses, from human space exploration to the possibility of alien beings and even alien visitations. In the past two decades, humans have progressed from taking short hops into orbit to living there for months on end. Humans have shown that they belong in space; they can live and work there as successfully as on Earth. In another two decades we could see the first child conceived and born in space. By next century, people could be spending their entire lives off Earth.

Whether or not life off Earth exists now, it will do so in centuries to come. Life off Earth will be human life.

Chapter One

FIRST IN SPACE

April 12, 1961. A squat, white and green rocket shaped like an upturned ice-cream cone stood on a concrete platform on the flat plains of central Russia outside the town of Tyuratam, 240 kilometres northeast of the Aral Sea. A spring breeze rippled the grass of the steppe as a small bus drove towards the rocket. In the bus were two men wearing rounded white helmets and loose-fitting orange coveralls over a modified jet pilot's pressure suit. One of these men was to go where no man had gone before – on a journey that would take him off the Earth and into space.

He was Yuri Alekseyevich Gagarin, a 27-year-old fighter pilot, the son of a farm labourer from Smolensk. The other man was his backup pilot, Herman Titov. The two had gone through every step of the final preparations together, but only Gagarin would take his place in the capsule at the top of the rocket 30 metres above them. Titov's turn would come on the next flight.

Technicians helped Gagarin and Titov out of the bus at the foot of the rocket. The two cosmonauts briefly embraced, and Gagarin made his departure speech to the small group of dignitaries who had gathered there in strict secrecy. The launch attempt was not announced until Gagarin was safely in orbit, in contrast to the widely publicized American manned launches that were to come later.

The formalities over, Gagarin stepped into the elevator that bore him to his capsule at the tip of the rocket. With a final wave to those on the ground below, he clambered on to the couch inside the spacecraft, and the hatch was closed. Ahead lay one of the greatest moments in the history of exploration.

Gagarin's spacecraft was a hermetically sealed steel sphere 2.3 metres in diameter, called Vostok. It contained normal Earth air at full atmospheric pressure. The air was supplied from small gas bottles around the base of the sphere, which contained enough to keep a man alive in space for up to 10 days.

Inside, the sphere was rather bare. It contained a minimum of instrumentation, for the Vostok cosmonaut was little more than an experimental passenger in an automatic satellite. Gagarin faced a small instrument panel with dials indicating the pressure, temperature and humidity, as well as a globe to show his position over the Earth. At his feet was a porthole containing an optical device known as Vzor for checking the orientation of the capsule. An insulating material coated the outside of the sphere to protect it from the fiery heat of re-entry into the Earth's atmosphere.

Prior to Gagarin's flight, five test launches of Vostoks had been made, carrying dummy cosmonauts and dogs. The final precursor was a dog named Zvezdochka (Little Star), a name given to her by Yuri Gagarin. On March 25, 1961, she performed one orbit of the Earth in a direct rehearsal of the mission that Gagarin was to undertake less than three weeks later.

Vostok 1 prepares for take off (right); no doubt an anxious time for Yuri Gagarin, soon to become the first man in space, cramped in a small hermetically sealed steel sphere, with only a tiny window on the world. An actor (above) portrays the daring cosmonaut at the instrument panel in the Soviet film The Space Test Pilot.

A Soviet cosmonaut briefly experiences weightlessness in a laboratory plane as it flies in a parabolic curve – like a giant roller coaster.

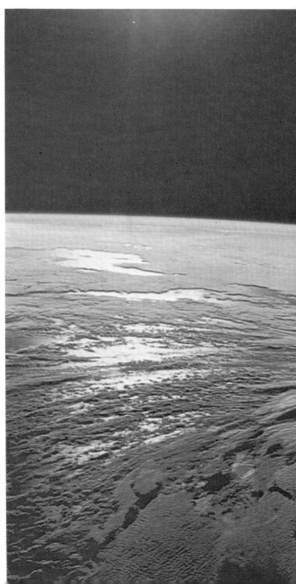

From space astronauts can see the beauty of our planet home with its life-giving air and water.

Remarkably enough, Zvezdochka's launch was the first time that Gagarin and his fellow Vostok cosmonauts visited the launch site and saw the rocket that was to propel them into space. By contrast, American spacemen were closely involved with the design and testing of their spacecraft and rockets.

In his Vostok capsule, Gagarin reported that all was well to launch control, situated in an underground concrete blockhouse near the launch pad. 'Your pulse rate is 64, and your respiration is 24,' launch control reported. 'Roger', replied Gagarin, 'so my heart is beating.' It was soon to beat faster in the excitement of launch.

'We're off,' shouted Gagarin as the rocket broke free of its restraining clamps and rose into the air. The roar was no louder than he was used to in the cockpit of a jet plane, but the tone of the engines was noticeably different. 'I got the impression that the powerful rocket engines were creating the music of the future,' he later said.

If the rocket had malfunctioned during launch, an ejector seat would have propelled him to safety. But all went well. As the rocket thundered into the sky the acceleration forces, known as g (for gravity) forces, pressed Gagarin into his seat as though a big hand were pressing down on his chest, making him six times heavier than on Earth. Like all spacemen, he had been trained to withstand such forces by being swung around in a centrifuge.

Then, as the upper stage of the rocket pushed Gagarin into an orbit ranging between 181 kilometres and 327 kilometres above the Earth's surface, the sensations changed. Instead of being heavy, he became weightless.

Weightlessness, also known as zero gravity, occurs in space because the spacecraft and its occupants are falling in a continual orbit around the Earth or other body; hence weightlessness is also termed free fall. During training, spacemen were able to experience weightlessness briefly aboard aeroplanes flying in a parabolic curve, like being on a roller coaster. But Gagarin was the first

to be weightless for any length of time. How well he withstood it would determine whether humans had a future in space.

Gagarin practised eating, drinking and writing during his flight. In weightlessness, these simple activities become a problem. For the early flights, food came in the form of a nutritious paste which was squeezed from a tube into the spaceman's mouth, while water was squirted from a pipe. Even before his flight, Gagarin had been put on a diet of space food from a tube and he found it satisfactory, if not exactly mouth-watering. While writing down his impressions in orbit, Gagarin momentarily forgot about the effect of weightlessness and laid down his pencil. It floated away under his seat where he could not retrieve it. His remaining notes were dictated into a tape recorder.

To his delight, the Earth and sky looked indescribably beautiful from orbit. On the night-time side of the Earth, he reported, the stars were clearly visible and the sky was blacker than it ever appears from the ground. When the Sun rose it did so abruptly, the fierce light stabbing into his eyes. He could see the farmlands of his home country below, and was able to distinguish ploughed fields from meadows. Scientists were astounded by detail visible to the eye from orbit; later spacemen reported seeing individual ships, aircraft vapour trails, roads and railways.

All too soon, it seemed, Gagarin's pioneer orbit of the Earth was coming to an end. Ahead of him was the most dangerous part of the mission – re-entry through the Earth's atmosphere and landing. Automatic systems on board Vostok aligned the spacecraft for re-entry and fired a retro-rocket to slow the sphere down. As the spacecraft dropped back into the atmosphere under the pull of Earth's gravity, Gagarin felt the g-forces build up once more, this time even stronger than during launch, because the capsule was being rapidly decelerated by the atmosphere. He watched apprehensively as red-hot flames licked past the spaceship's windows. But despite the searing heat outside the craft caused by friction with the dense layers of the Earth's atmosphere, Vostok's surface insulation kept the inside of the craft at a comfortable 20°C.

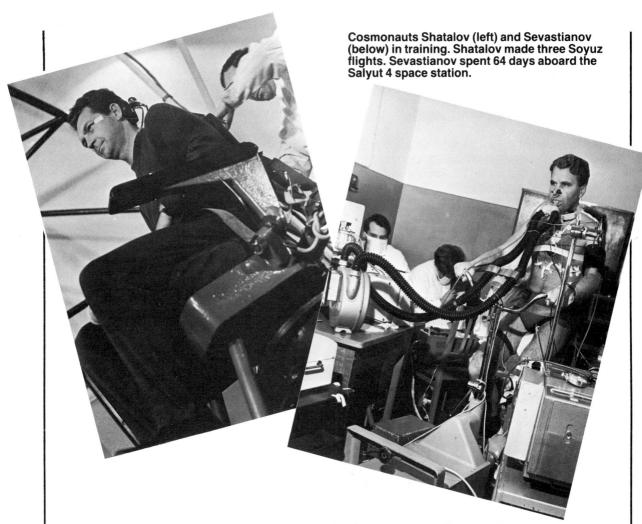

Cosmonauts Shatalov (left) and Sevastianov (below) in training. Shatalov made three Soyuz flights. Sevastianov spent 64 days aboard the Salyut 4 space station.

At an altitude of 7 kilometres Gagarin ejected from the capsule and landed by parachute in a ploughed field of a collective farm near Saratov, much to the surprise of a forester's wife and her granddaughter who were planting potatoes there. Gagarin's bright orange coverall made him easily visible to the recovery crews who arrived by helicopter shortly afterwards. The total flight, from launch to landing, had lasted 108 minutes.

The world was astounded by Gagarin's daring feat. Only a few years previously it had been feared that a spaceman might be seared by radiation or peppered by tiny meteorites as soon as he emerged above the protective layers of the Earth's atmosphere. Satellites had shown those fears to be unfounded, but

doctors were still worried about the effects of weightlessness on a human. Various dire effects were predicted, such as that the spacemen would become disoriented, and that there would be changes in normal bodily functions.

Reassuringly, Gagarin reported no significant problems. 'When I became weightless I felt perfectly well,' he said later. 'I was not sitting in my chair as before – I hung in the air. My handwriting did not change, even though the hand was weightless. Weightlessness did not affect my capacity to work.'

Gagarin had shown that weightlessness could be conquered, at least for one orbit of the Earth. But what about longer flights? On August 6, 1961, Herman Titov was lofted into space aboard Vostok 2 for a complete day, during which he would circle the Earth 17 times, seeing the Sun rise and set every 90 minutes. And it was on this mission that the first medical problems surfaced.

During his second orbit, Titov began to feel nausea, particularly when turning his head or watching moving objects. This was the first appearance of so-called space sickness, which has proved to be the most common and upsetting side effect of manned spaceflight.

Space sickness is akin to travel sickness experienced in cars, ships and aircraft. The problem stems from the sensitive balancing mechanism in the inner ear which informs the brain about the head's movements. On Earth, symptoms of sickness are caused by unfamiliar motion of cars, ships and planes in the Earth's gravitational field; but in space it is the lack of gravity that is the problem, so that an astronaut who moves his head around will feel sick. In both environments, the brain receives confused signals from the inner ear's sensors, but exactly why this should result in stomach sickness remains a mystery. Fortunately, the brain soon learns to cope with the new sensations of motion, both on Earth and in space.

American spacemen did not suffer space sickness until the start of the Apollo series, probably because Apollo was the first craft that gave them any room to move about in. Some people are more prone to space sickness than others, for reasons yet to be explained. At present there is no way of telling in advance who is most likely to suffer.

Titov's appetite was affected by his space sickness, but nevertheless he did his best to consume his first space lunch, consisting of a puree squeezed from a tube like a toothpaste tube, meat paté, squares of bread and blackcurrant juice. After his sixth orbit Titov settled down to sleep, securing his hands so they would not float up in front of him. On awakening, most of the unpleasant space-sickness sensations had disappeared, and he prevented them from returning by avoiding any sudden movements of the head. He breakfasted and completed the flight without further incident, although on landing he reported other symptoms that later spacemen were to experience: dizziness and unsteadi-

ness when standing, as his blood redistributed itself into the lower part of his body and his balancing mechanism readjusted to functioning in Earth's gravity. These feelings soon passed.

Although there were no long-term ill effects from the mission, Soviet space doctors were sufficiently concerned by Titov's experience to intensify the training programme of the other cosmonauts. In the meantime, American astronauts had begun their own series of space flights in spacecraft called Mercury.

The Mercury capsule was conical in shape, 2.9 metres long and just over 1.8 metres wide at the base where the heat shield was located. Atop the spacecraft was a rocket-controlled escape tower that would have pulled it to safety in the event of a launch emergency. Mercury astronauts were crammed inside their capsule with their spacesuit helmet touching one wall and their feet against another. It was a tight fit, and not for the claustrophobic; but these men were jet fighter pilots, used to small cockpits. Unlike Soviet spacecraft which used normal Earth air of nitrogen and oxygen at sea-level pressure, Mercury, Gemini and Apollo spacecraft used an atmosphere of pure oxygen at one-third atmospheric pressure. This made for a simpler, lighter spacecraft.

The astronaut sat in a couch contoured to his body shape. In front of his face was a control panel with, centrally placed, a viewing window for a periscope. Above him was an observation window in the spacecraft hatch. He had hand controls which could turn the spacecraft while in orbit. After re-entry, parachutes emerged from the capsule's nose and the craft with the astronaut aboard splashed down in the ocean.

The first two Mercury flights were brief up-and-down lobs that took the astronauts above the atmosphere but not into orbit. Not until the third flight did John Glenn become the first American to orbit the Earth, circling the globe three times on February 20, 1962. The longest Mercury flight was the sixth and last, in May 1963, when L. Gordon Cooper stayed aloft for 22 orbits lasting 34 hours. During his extended mission Cooper sampled improved space food consisting of 'bite-sized'

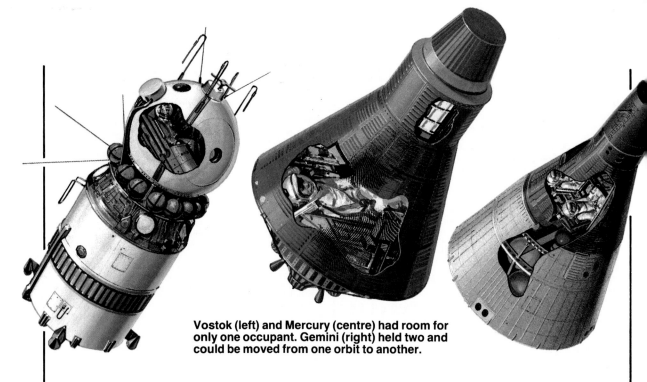

Vostok (left) and Mercury (centre) had room for only one occupant. Gemini (right) held two and could be moved from one orbit to another.

solid chunks, and pouches of dehydrated soups and stews that were reconstituted by adding water. He released a flashing beacon and watched it to judge how well objects could be seen in space, information that would be of use in later missions when two spacecraft approached and docked.

So fast was the space race developing that by the time of Cooper's flight the Russians had taken a further leap ahead, putting two Vostoks in orbit at once. Andrian Nikolayev took off first in Vostok 3 on August 11, 1962, for a flight lasting 4 days during which he completed 64 orbits. The following day Pavel Popovich was launched in Vostok 4, entering orbit about 6.5 kilometres from his space twin, close enough for the two to see each other. Without manoeuvring engines, the Vostoks subsequently drifted apart, but such close launchings would be vital for later attempts at docking between improved craft.

There was one more surprise before the Vostok programme concluded. On June 14, 1963, Valery Bykovsky set off in Vostok 5 for what remains the longest-ever solo spaceflight: 81 orbits, lasting 119 hours. Two days later came the real sensation when the first space woman, Valentina Tereshkova, was launched in Vostok 6. Unlike the other cosmonauts who had all been Air Force fighter pilots, Valentina was a civilian whose hobby was parachute jumping. A woman in space had clear biological interest, but there was also a propaganda angle in Valentina's 48-orbit flight.

One additional, unplanned biological experiment occurred later that year when Valentina married cosmonaut Andrian Nikolayev; the two had been living together in the cosmonauts' village. Seven months after the wedding Valentina gave birth to a healthy baby girl. This finally disposed of any worries that radiation in space would cause genetic damage, a fear which had prompted a number of the early American astronauts to have vasectomies.

As the next step along the road to the Moon, the United States planned a series of two-man spacecraft called Gemini. There was consternation in Soviet space circles because their new spacecraft, Soyuz, would not be ready in time to meet this challenge. So a stop-gap solution was devised. Vostok had its ejector seat ripped out and not two but three men were crammed into the sphere originally intended for one. The craft was renamed Voskhod. The Soviet Union boasted that it provided a 'shirt-sleeve' environment. But the truth was that in the impossibly cramped conditions there was no room for the three men to wear spacesuits. Without ejector seats or spacesuits, the helpless crew had to hope that the rocket would not malfunction during launch, and that once in space the craft would not spring a leak. Voskhod was a desperate risk – but it worked.

On October 12, 1964, Voskhod 1 was launched carrying Vladimir Komarov, a cosmonaut from the original batch who had not yet flown, Konstantin Feoktistov, a spacecraft designer, and Boris Yegorov, a space doctor. To a startled world, it appeared as though the Soviet Union had jumped two stages ahead of the Americans. Voskhod's crew spent what must have been an uncomfortable day in space, performing 16 orbits of the Earth. Both Feoktistov and Yegorov had had only a few months training for the mission, and both suffered badly from space sickness.

Despite the risks, Voskhod 1 returned safely. Braking rockets allowed the capsule to soft-land with the crew still on board. The mission was hailed as a triumph, even though it was scarcely any advance on the flight of Titov three years before. But the next flight did break new ground. Voskhod 2 took off on March 18, 1965, carrying two cosmonauts in spacesuits. One of the men, Alexei Leonov, was to crawl through a tiny airlock to make the first walk in space.

This airlock was a telescopic affair folded down against one of the hatches of the modified Vostok. Once in orbit, the airlock was extended and pressurized. Leonov squeezed into it, shut the spacecraft hatch behind him, then opened the outer door on the airlock. He was free, floating in space like a human satellite, connected to Voskhod 2 by a five-metre tether but breathing from air supplies on his back like a diver.

Leonov's space walk dispelled fears that space walkers might become disoriented in the black emptiness of space. For ten minutes he moved around outside the craft, on one occasion turning joyous somersaults. He and the spacecraft were orbiting the Earth at 28,000 km/h but he had no sensation of speed. 'When I looked at the capsule it seemed to be hanging motionless in the cosmic abyss,' Leonov said. Inside Voskhod 2, pilot Pavel

Belyayev could feel the spacecraft move as Leonov pushed against it, and even heard the clang of his space boot as it scraped the outside. Moving around in the bulky, inflated spacesuit was tiring, and the sweating Leonov had to let some of the air out of his suit before he could bend sufficiently to squeeze back into the airlock after his space walk.

Even then, the alarms were not over. On the 17th orbit the spacecraft should have automatically aligned itself for re-entry, prior to the firing of the retro-rockets. But Belyayev and Leonov found to their horror that the attitude control system had failed. They went once more around the Earth, their 18th orbit, and then aligned the ship manually for re-entry. On a signal from ground control, Belyayev fired the retro-rockets manually. He was still not satisfied that the craft was aligned correctly for re-entry, but he had no choice.

A slight error in alignment could have meant that the craft entered the atmosphere at too steep an angle and burned up. Fortunately, Voskhod 2 survived its fiery re-entry with only the loss of a radio communications aerial. But it came down 2,000 kilometres off target, in the middle of a forest on the snow-covered slopes of the Ural mountains. Helicopters dropped supplies to the cosmonauts, but they had to spend a chilly night fighting off wolves before being lifted to safety.

No further modifications could be made to the already stretched Vostok that would allow it to stand comparison with the American Gemini. After Leonov's space walk the risks were judged too great, and the stop-gap Voskhod was quietly retired. Although Vostok capsules and the subsequent Soyuz have been displayed publicly, the Soviet Union has never released any official drawings or models of Voskhod.

Four days after Voskhod 2 returned to Earth, the United States launched the first of its two-man Gemini craft. Gemini's purpose was to prove three things: that humans could endure weightlessness long enough for a round trip to the Moon; that spacecraft could find each cther in orbit and link up; and that humans could work successfully outside their spacecraft.

Gemini's crew compartment was like an enlarged version of Mercury. Behind it was an additional section containing electrical and air supplies, plus retro-rockets; this section was jettisoned before re-entry. Gemini's two astronauts sat side by side in ejector seats which would have shot them to safety if the launch rocket malfunctioned. Above each man was a hatch with a small half-moon shaped window.

Gemini had small steering jets in its nose and flanks, enabling it to change orbit and to link with other craft. No longer were astronauts mere guinea pigs; now they would act like true pilots, manoeuvring their craft in space. In the craft's nose was a radar, coupled to a computer on the astronaut's instrument panel which governed rendezvous and docking manoeuvres.

For all its advanced features, Gemini was still cramped; sitting in it was like being in the front seat of a small car. Fortunately, in weightlessness one is not really 'sitting' at all but floating, so it's possible to remain in such a confined position for days on end without too much discomfort.

After two unmanned test flights, a two-stage Titan rocket propelled Gemini 3 skywards on March 23, 1965, from Cape Canaveral. Aboard was Virgil 'Gus' Grissom, veteran of the second Mercury sub-orbital flight and thus the first man to go into space twice; with him was John Young, who made an unscheduled addition to the normal space menu by smuggling aboard a corned beef sandwich. Gemini 3 orbited the Earth, firing its steering jets to become the first manned spacecraft to change orbit.

Next came a far more ambitious flight. Gemini 4, commanded by James McDivitt, would complete a four-day, 62-orbit flight; but more importantly, during the flight Edward White would emerge to perform the first American walk in space. Gemini did not have an airlock, so the entire craft was depressurized and the hatch opened.

White wore a seven-layer spacesuit, consisting of cotton and nylon undergarments, a nylon pressure suit, a strengthening layer to prevent the suit ballooning out of shape, a heat insulating layer consisting of aluminium-coated plastic film, a protecting layer against micrometeorites, and a nylon top covering. A pressurized spacesuit is a very cumbersome garment. One astronaut described it as like wearing five or six overcoats and pairs of gloves at once. McDivitt, inside the spacecraft, wore a simpler suit without the layers for micrometeorite protection and heat insulation.

'Absolutely no disorientation and no sensation of falling,' White reported to relieved space doctors as he made his spacewalk during Gemini 4's third orbit on June 3, 1965. Connecting him to the spacecraft was a 7.6-metre umbilical cord, through which oxygen flowed. White used a hand-held jet gun to push himself around outside the craft, enjoying himself so much that he was reluctant to come in again. White stayed outside the spacecraft for 21 minutes, twice as long as Leonov had done.

Of all the vital human processes that a spacecraft has to support, the most awkward is waste disposal. How do astronauts go to the toilet? The answer is: with some difficulty. Urination is accomplished relatively straightforwardly, into a pipe and through a valve overboard or into a collecting tank, although there have been embarrassing spillages. Solid wastes are more difficult. Some astronauts preferred to take medicines to delay the dreaded moment for as long as possible, preferably until they were back on the ground. But on missions lasting more than a few days there was really no alternative.

The basic sanitary appliance for Gemini and Apollo was a plastic bag with an adhesive rim which the astronaut stuck to his buttocks for defecation. In weightlessness there is no particular reason for the waste to drop into the bag, so a finger stall was provided at the side of the bag for the astronaut to help separate the waste from his body. After use the bag was sealed and kneaded to mix in a germicide that prevented gas forming. The bag was then stored for analysis. The whole performance could take as much as an hour.

McDivitt and White in Gemini 4 extended American spaceflight experience to four days' duration. Gemini 5 doubled this, surpassing the longest Russian flight of Valery

Bykovsky. During Gemini 5's 120-orbit mission in August 1965, Gordon Cooper and Pete Conrad carried out numerous experiments, including photography of the Earth revealing astounding detail visible from on high. So good was the astronauts' condition on their return that chief American space doctor Charles Berry decided next to aim for a 14-day mission. It was accomplished by Gemini 7 which, by a quirk of fate, was launched before Gemini 6.

Gemini 6 had been intended to dock with a modified Agena rocket, but the mission was cancelled after the Agena failed to make it into orbit. Instead, Gemini 7's launch was brought forward and Gemini 6 was sent up to rendezvous with it. For eight hours on the afternoon of December 15, 1965, Gemini 6 piloted by Walter Schirra and Tom Stafford manoeuvred to within 30 centimetres of Gemini 7, containing Frank Borman and James Lovell, in an impressive piece of formation flying. Its job done, Gemini 6 returned to Earth leaving Borman and Lovell to complete their record-breaking 206-orbit mission.

For comfort during their extended flight Borman and Lovell were equipped with new lightweight spacesuits, but for much of the time they removed even these and flew in their 'long john' underwear. Both men took books to read but in the event they were kept so busy with the rendezvous and 20 other experiments that neither got a chance to finish them.

Considerable medical information came out of this mission. Previously it had been found that astronauts' muscles and bones weaken in weightlessness, for they no longer have to work against the pull of Earth's gravity. In an attempt to prevent these effects building up, the Gemini 7 astronauts exercised their legs and arms by pulling on rubber cords each day. They were strong enough to stand when they emerged onto the deck of the recovery ship.

Gemini 8 in March 1966 performed the first space docking when Neil Armstrong and David Scott caught up with an Agena target vehicle and, using careful bursts from Gemini's thrusters, guided the Gemini's extended nose into a docking collar on the Agena. Then trouble struck. One of the spacecraft's thrusters stuck open, sending the Gemini-Agena combination into a dangerous spin. With the presence of mind of an experienced test pilot, Armstrong backed off from the Agena and shut down the offending thruster. In view of the problem, ground control decided to bring the astronauts back to Earth immediately.

By then, the Gemini programme was well into its stride. Flights of increasing complexity were undertaken. Gemini 9 astronaut Eugene Cernan left his spacecraft for a 2-hour spacewalk, known in NASA jargon as an EVA (extravehicular activity). He had to move around behind Gemini where he put on the Astronaut Manoeuvring Unit, a jet-propelled backpack with arm rests in which were mounted controls. But Cernan found the effort of moving around in space to be greater than anticipated. His exertions in attempting to strap on the manoeuvring unit caused his spacesuit to overheat, and his visor fogged up so he could hardly see where he was going. The spacewalk was abandoned and he returned to the cabin, sweating profusely.

Michael Collins on Gemini 10 encountered similar difficulties when he spacewalked across to an Agena target vehicle to retrieve a meteorite impact detector, and so did Richard Gordon on Gemini 11 when he attached a tether to an Agena. The problem for the astronaut was keeping himself in position while floating in weightlessness. His every action tended to push him in the opposite direction, and once moving it was difficult to stop again. So the astronaut spent most of his time floundering around in a bulky and unresponsive spacesuit.

Despite the difficulties with EVA, both these Gemini flights accomplished their docking objectives, including using the Agena to boost themselves to record altitudes up to 1350 kilometres above the Earth. Gemini 11 also experienced slight artificial gravity when it began a deliberate cartwheel motion with the Agena to which Richard Gordon had tethered it.

The problems of walking and working in space were finally overcome on the last and most successful mission, Gemini 12. On this four-day, 59-orbit flight, Edwin 'Buzz' Aldrin left his cabin for a record 2½-hour EVA, first moving across to the Agena and then clambering around to the rear of the Gemini. His mobility was aided by two things. Firstly, he had trained extensively in a water tank on Earth in which the buoyancy of the water reproduces the effect of weightlessness and he was therefore much better prepared for his tasks than previous space walkers. Underwater training became standard for later astronauts. Secondly, the Gemini and Agena were fitted with numerous handholds and footholds, and Aldrin wore a harness which he could clip to the spacecraft where he was working to help keep him in place. In a work station at the rear of Gemini 12 he practised using various tools, including wire cutters and a wrench for turning bolts.

Gemini 12's splashdown on November 15, 1966, brought the series to a triumphant close. Humans had shown that they could live and work successfully in space for extended periods. Weightlessness turned out to be an enjoyable experience, something to which astronauts became adjusted with no deleterious effects after they returned to Earth. Although space was an alien environment, humans belonged in it. All was now set for an even bigger step – the Moon.

Chapter Two

ON THE MOON

A challenge that would change the world was laid down in May 1961, shortly after the start of the Mercury programme, by US President John F. Kennedy: to land a man on the Moon and return him safely to Earth before the decade of the 1960s was out. It was a goal both technically demanding and yet deeply romantic, appealing to an age-old desire of mankind. At last, humans from planet Earth would set foot on another body in space.

It was also, quite frankly, politically motivated. The United States, self-appointed technological leaders of the world, had been stung by the repeated reversals visited upon them by the first Russian Sputnik and then the first Russian man in space. The Moon, it seemed, was the only worthwhile prize which they could be assured of reaching before the Russians. But how to do it?

There were conflicting ideas. One involved landing an entire three-man Apollo spacecraft on the Moon. Fortunately, there was a simpler alternative. Three men would be launched to the Moon in an Apollo, but only two would make lunar landfall. A smaller, separate craft would detach from the Apollo mother ship in orbit around the Moon, take two men to the lunar surface and return them to the mother ship before being discarded.

For the Moon missions a giant new spaceport was built in the Florida swamp at Cape Canaveral, consisting of two identical launch pads and a voluminous construction hangar, the Vehicle Assembly Building, in which Saturn V rockets were assembled before being transported to the pad. NASA took 32,000 hectares of Florida wilderness to build this spaceport. The Vehicle Assembly Building (VAB), one of the largest buildings in the world, enclosed 3.7 million cubic metres of space, had to be air conditioned to prevent clouds forming within it, and was tied down with deep pile foundations to prevent it from blowing away like a box kite in strong winds. The top of the VAB, 160 metres up, was the highest point in Florida.

Inside the VAB the three stages of each Saturn V, the world's largest and most powerful rocket, were stacked on top of each other like building blocks. Standing 111 metres high, the Saturn V weighed 200 tonnes empty but could contain 15 times its own weight in fuel. At lift-off its first stage produced a thrust of nearly 3500 tonnes.

At the tip of Saturn V was the Apollo spacecraft itself, the home for three astronauts during their trip to the Moon and back. Surmounting it was a rocket-propelled escape tower to pull it to safety if the Saturn V malfunctioned at launch. Apollo's command module was a cone 3.5 metres high and nearly 4 metres in diameter. Inside it, the three astronauts sat side by side. Banks of switches, lights and dials faced them 60 centimetres in front of their eyes. The astronauts slept in their seats or in sleeping bags slung under the couches. To most people Apollo looks pretty cramped, but by comparison with Gemini it was luxurious – there was even room to stand up.

At the apex of the command module was a docking probe and hatch through which crewmembers could crawl into another spacecraft. Stacked around this circular hatch were three parachutes under which the craft would descend to a gentle splashdown in the Pacific at journey's end. To protect against the intense heat of re-entry at 40,000 km/h into the Earth's atmosphere the Apollo command module was encased in a heat shield of stainless steel honeycomb with a reinforced plastic coating. The plastic coating was designed to melt and flow away, taking the re-entry heat with it. At the base of Apollo, where heating

The dinky-sized cars give an idea of the immense height of the Saturn V rocket and the giant Vehicle Assembly Building (VAB).

would be greatest, the thickness of the heat-shield was over 6.3 centimetres, tapering to 2.5 centimetres near the apex.

Behind the command module was the cylindrical service module containing supplies of air and electricity-generating fuel cells, plus the large engine that would fire for the crucial manoeuvres of putting Apollo into orbit around the Moon and sending it safely home again. By early 1967, all seemed ready for Apollo's first test flight around the Earth. But the Apollo programme was to exact a terrible price before success was eventually achieved.

'We're on fire! Get us out of here!' Those were the desperate last words from the crew intended to fly the first manned Apollo. During a practice countdown on January 27, 1967, atop the rocket that should have taken them into orbit less than a month later, fire broke out, apparently because of a spark from faulty wiring insulation. Fed by the pure oxygen atmosphere and combustible materials such as plastics, the fire rapidly spread. Smoke got into the astronauts' spacesuits, suffocating them within 30 seconds while they still frantically tried to escape. But the tightly sealed Apollo hatch was unyielding. Gus Grissom, Ed White and Roger Chaffee were dead long before ground crews could get close to help them.

It was a stunning tragedy. The Apollo programme was halted for over a year while the craft was redesigned, eliminating the faults that had led to the electrical spark and replacing flammable materials with fireproof ones. A new quick-release hatch was installed.

That was not the only space tragedy to strike in 1967. In April of that year the Soviet Union test-flew the first of its new-generation spaceships called Soyuz, piloted by Voskhod 1 veteran Vladimir Komarov. Soyuz is a three-part craft: a central bullet-shaped crew compartment with behind it a cylindrical service module and at the front a spherical compartment to provide additional living and working accommodation while in orbit. Soyuz is 7.2 metres long overall; its diameter is just over 2 metres, very nearly the same as Vostok.

Things soon went wrong with Soyuz on its maiden flight. The craft reportedly proved difficult to control, and Komarov made an emergency landing after 18 orbits. But the parachute lines of the spinning spacecraft became entangled, and Soyuz 1 with Komarov aboard crashed into the steppes of central Asia. It was another tragic reminder of the dangers that still lurked aboard every spaceflight.

Apollo got into action in October 1968 with a perfect 11-day flight by Walter Schirra, Donn Eisele and Walter Cunningham who thoroughly checked out the redesigned spacecraft, particularly the large engine on which the astronauts would depend when far from Earth. Apollo 7 had been launched by the Saturn IB, smaller brother of the Saturn V. The next launch was to be the first time that humans rode the monster Saturn V.

The pace of the space race was stepping up again. A week after Apollo 7 returned to Earth, the Russians successfully test flew their redesigned Soyuz with Georgi Beregovoi aboard. In September and November 1968 the Russians sent unmanned Soyuz, called Zond, on looping paths around the Moon and back again, and there were fears that they might try to steal Apollo's glory by putting a man in the next one. So on December 21, the thunderous roar of a Saturn V rent the air at Cape Canaveral as the crew of Apollo 8 departed not merely into orbit around the Earth, as had originally been intended, but to circle the Moon.

After 2½ minutes the first stage of the rocket, its fuel consumed, fell away at a height of 64 kilometres, having reached a speed in excess of 9600 km/h. Then the second stage took over for 6 minutes, pushing the rocket and spacecraft to an altitude of 185 kilometres and a speed of 24,000 km/h. Then it, too, fell away, leaving the third stage. Less than 12 minutes after lift-off Apollo 8 was safely in parking orbit 190 kilometres above the Earth, moving at 28,000 km/h.

Aboard were Frank Borman and James Lovell, veterans of the Gemini 7 marathon, and new astronaut Bill Anders. Two orbits later, having checked that the spacecraft had come safely through its launch, the rocket's third stage was ignited again, pushing Apollo 8 towards the Moon at a speed of 38,600 km/h.

Briefly they passed through the Van Allen radiation belts surrounding the Earth, receiving a radiation dose no stronger than that used for a dental X-ray. For all his spaceflight experience, Borman suffered space sickness and vomited twice on his second day in space. This may have been due in part to a sleeping pill and also gastric flu which had been sweeping the Cape before launch. Whatever the cause, the sickness soon passed.

Three days later, Borman, Lovell and Anders became the first humans to be captured by the gravity of another world. The big engine at the rear of Apollo's service module fired to place them in orbit ranging from 320 kilometres to 112 kilometres above the Moon's surface. For 20 hours they orbited the Moon, describing its surface as 'like dirty beach sand, with lots of footprints' and taking photographs of potential landing sites. Ten times they orbited the Moon before firing their service module's engine again to bring them safely back to a splashdown in the Pacific on December 27. After Apollo 8, all Soviet interest in manned Moon flight vanished.

One important Apollo component remained to be tested before men could land on the Moon: the lunar module in which two astronauts would actually touch down. The lunar module (LM) came in two halves, standing a total 7 metres tall. The lower half contained four landing legs and a large engine for the LM's descent to the surface. Astronauts rode in the top half of the LM, supported by harnesses as they stood at the LM's controls. On the Moon the lower half of the LM was used as a launching pad for the top half, which had a separate engine to boost the astronauts from the lunar surface to rejoin the command module orbiting above. Then even this top stage was discarded.

Because the LM was intended to operate only in the vacuum of space it was not streamlined. Its lumpy, spidery shape gave rise to its nickname of the Moonbug. At launch it travelled below the command and service modules.

Apollo 9 put the ugly Moonbug through its paces in the comparative safety of orbit around the Earth. Once in orbit, astronauts

James McDivitt, David Scott and Russell Schweickart turned their command and service modules to dock with the Moonbug and draw it out from the top of the Saturn V's third stage in which it nestled. Then McDivitt and Schweickart crawled through the docking hatch into the lunar module and broke away from the command module. Discarding the bottom half of the LM they returned in the top half to dock with the command module, as though they had just come back from a lunar landing. All went well.

During this flight Schweickart tried out the new Apollo Moon suit for the first time in space. On the fourth day of the mission Schweickart stood on the porch of the lunar module for 40 minutes, relying on his suit alone for survival. 'Very comfortable,' was his verdict. Schweickart should have spent longer on his EVA but he had experienced recurrent bouts of space sickness. He first vomited unexpectedly while putting on his pressure suit, but fortunately kept his mouth shut until he could reach a disposal bag. He later vomited again and never felt fully well all the time he was in space. He was the only astronaut never to adapt fully to weightlessness.

Learning from experience gained during Gemini EVAs when astronauts overheated, NASA's designers included a water-cooled undergarment in Schweickart's suit. Water was pumped through plastic pipes to carry heat away from his body. To the back of the Moon suit was strapped a pack which provided the cooling water, plus oxygen for Schweickart to breathe. This back pack, known in NASA jargon as the Portable Life Support System (PLSS), turned the Moon suit into a portable spacecraft.

One of the most difficult requirements for the Moon suit was a glove that was flexible and transmitted some sense of touch, while insulating the astronaut against the extremes of hot and cold when handling objects on the Moon. EVA gloves were individually moulded from casts of each astronaut's hands and shaped by metal bars along natural folds. Flexible joints allowed movement at knuckles and wrist, and fingers were tipped by silicone rubber. Special ankle joints were needed too, or else the pressure of the

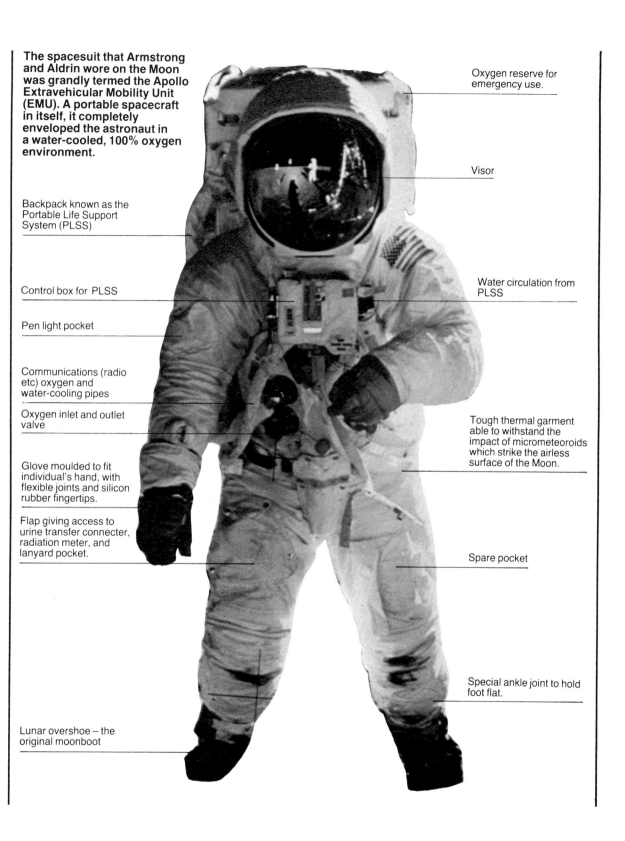

The spacesuit that Armstrong and Aldrin wore on the Moon was grandly termed the Apollo Extravehicular Mobility Unit (EMU). A portable spacecraft in itself, it completely enveloped the astronaut in a water-cooled, 100% oxygen environment.

Oxygen reserve for emergency use.

Visor

Backpack known as the Portable Life Support System (PLSS)

Water circulation from PLSS

Control box for PLSS

Pen light pocket

Communications (radio etc) oxygen and water-cooling pipes

Oxygen inlet and outlet valve

Tough thermal garment able to withstand the impact of micrometeoroids which strike the airless surface of the Moon.

Glove moulded to fit individual's hand, with flexible joints and silicon rubber fingertips.

Flap giving access to urine transfer connecter, radiation meter, and lanyard pocket.

Spare pocket

Special ankle joint to hold foot flat.

Lunar overshoe – the original moonboot

inflated suit would have extended the foot so that the astronaut was walking along on his toes. Simpler spacesuits were worn inside the craft, fed with oxygen from spacecraft supplies.

The time had come for a dress rehearsal of the first lunar landing. This task fell to Apollo 10, launched towards the Moon on May 18, 1969. Entering orbit around the Moon three days later, Tom Stafford and Eugene Cernan, colleagues from Gemini 9, crawled into the lunar module nicknamed Snoopy, leaving John Young in the command module, call sign Charlie Brown. Using the lunar module's descent engine, Stafford and Cernan swooped down to within 15 kilometres of the Moon's surface.

'We're right there! We're right over it!' exclaimed Cernan ecstatically as he looked down on the intended Apollo 11 landing site in the Sea of Tranquillity, a flat lunar lowland. 'We are low. We're close, babe,' he gasped. Stafford described the landing site as 'very smooth, like a dry riverbed in New Mexico or Arizona.' Of course, there never has been any water on the Moon, but Stafford's description confirmed the smoothness and hence the safety of the intended landing site.

To their regret, they were not scheduled to make that first touchdown. Instead, the flight plan called for them to separate the two halves of the lunar module and return to the command ship. But as the lunar module's lower stage was jettisoned, the upper stage began to vibrate like a bucking bronco. 'Son of a bitch!' Cernan exclaimed in alarm. 'I thought we were wobbling all over the sky,' he added as Stafford brought the LM under control. The trouble was attributed to a guidance system for locating the command module which should not have been switched on.

Using the LM's ascent stage engine, Stafford and Cernan rode back to the command module as though returning from the surface of the Moon. 'Snoopy and Charlie Brown are hugging each other,' declared a delighted Stafford as the two craft docked.

On the way back to Earth, the astronauts demonstrated 'scientific experiment Sugar Hotel Alpha Victor Echo.' NASA had put much effort into designing an electric razor for space use that sucked up cut bristles with a built-in vacuum cleaner. But these contraptions never performed successfully – and in the event they proved unnecessary. The Apollo 10 astronauts demonstrated that it was perfectly possible to wet shave in space. Using a tube of conventional brushless shaving foam and a safety razor, they attacked their week-old stubble, wiping the razor with a towel after every stroke. The stubble adhered to the cream and never floated around in the cabin. Another problem of living in space was solved.

Apollo 10 returned home eight years and one day after President Kennedy laid down the goal of landing humans on the Moon. Within hours of their return, NASA announced that Apollo 11 would fulfil that challenge. Beings from the planet Earth would at last walk on the surface of another body in space.

An estimated million sightseers jammed the roads, beaches and riverfronts around Cape Canaveral on July 16, 1969, while hundreds of millions more watched on television around the world as Apollo 11 began its journey into history. The men of Apollo 11 were: Neil Armstrong, the commander, reserved, boyish, but a supremely skilful pilot of great courage, as he had displayed on the Gemini 8 flight; Michael Collins, command module pilot, good natured and easy going; Edwin 'Buzz' Aldrin, lunar module pilot, athletic, stylish, fiercely ambitious, with a computer-like brain.

After a preliminary one and a half laps around the Earth to check that all was well with the spacecraft, the third stage of the Saturn V rocket fired again to put Apollo 11 en route for the Moon. Half an hour later, the astronauts turned the main spaceship, codenamed Columbia, to dock with the lunar module, call sign Eagle. The third stage of the Saturn V then dumped its leftover fuel into space, propelling itself on to a new trajectory that would not interfere with Apollo 11.

Soon the crew were enjoying their first meal. Space food had come a long way since the days of Mercury. More than 70 different items made up the Apollo 11 crew's menu. Main-course delicacies included spaghetti

A tasty meal of freeze-dried beef stew – just add hot water and eat with a spoon – but don't let go of the spoon!

with meat sauce, chicken and rice, and turkey with gravy, followed by butterscotch pudding, fruit cocktail or pineapple fruitcake.

Food came in two main forms: ready-to-eat bite-sized chunks such as bacon squares and toast cubes, and bags of freeze-dried food to which water had to be added. Freeze-dried foods are first cooked, then immediately frozen in liquid nitrogen, and finally placed into a vacuum chamber and heated to drive off the ice in the food. The lunch-pot foods now available in supermarkets are made this way, so you may have eaten space-type food without realizing it.

Aboard Apollo, the freeze-dried foods were reconstituted by injecting hot water from a gun into the bag – an improvement over Gemini, in which only cold water was available. The bag was then kneaded for several minutes, the end cut off and the food squeezed into the astronaut's mouth. Hot and cold drinks were made up in similar fashion. Water is readily available on board American spacecraft because it is produced by the electricity-generating fuel cells. Dehydrated foods save weight and space, and are easier to store. A few foods on Apollo came in flexible foil pouches known as wetpacks. And some foods were sticky enough to be eaten with a spoon, a technique that has since entirely replaced the squeegee method of eating in space. After dining the astronauts wiped their hands with damp towels. They were also supplied with chewing gum, edible toothpaste, and toothbrushes.

Seventy-two hours after launch Apollo 11 was approaching the Moon. Earlier, the brilliance of the Earth made it impossible to see stars clearly, but that had now changed. 'We are able to recognize constellations for the first time on the trip,' reported Collins. Seventy-six hours into the mission Apollo 11 disappeared behind the Moon and used its on-board engine to put itself into orbit. The big moment was getting nearer.

After a day in lunar orbit, Armstrong and Aldrin crawled into the lunar module and separated it from the command module. 'The Eagle has wings,' radioed Armstrong. Then began their descent under control of the LM's radar and computer towards their intended landing site on the Sea of Tranquillity.

But as the landing site came into view the astronauts saw they were slightly off course and heading for a crater the size of a football field filled with large rocks. Armstrong took manual control, steering the craft to a smoother spot while Aldrin called out instrument readings of altitude and speed.

Through the Moonbug's triangular windows the astronauts saw the shadow of the LM's landing legs hovering over the dusty lunar surface. As fuel ran low, a light flashed on the instrument panel to indicate that probes below the Moonbug's footpads were brushing the surface. 'Contact light,' called Aldrin. Armstrong cut off the descent engine, and the lunar module dropped the last few feet to the surface.

'Tranquillity Base here. The Eagle has landed,' reported Armstrong. People watching and listening around the world let out a collective sigh of relief. Two men were on the Moon. It was 8.18 P.M. GMT, July 20, 1969.

In the confined space of the lunar module, Armstrong and Aldrin found it difficult to put on their PLSS backpacks. They were no longer weightless, but now had the weight of a two-stone infant – one-sixth their normal

Earth weight, because the Moon's gravity is one-sixth that of Earth.

Six and a half hours after landing, the hatch was opened at Tranquillity Base and Armstrong crawled on to the porch of the lunar module. He then began carefully to descend a ladder to the surface, pulling open a flap on the LM's side that exposed a television camera to monitor his activities. He halted at the last step, his shadowy form visible to TV watchers in their homes on Earth. A new world was being explored in the full gaze of the public.

'I'm at the foot of the ladder,' Armstrong said matter-of-factly. 'The LM footpads are only depressed in the surface about one or two inches. The surface appears to be very fine grained ... it's almost like a powder. I'm going to step off the LM now,' he announced. Armstrong put out his left foot and stood on the Moon. Inevitably, his first words would be historic: 'That's one small step for a man; one giant leap for mankind.' It was a moment in evolution as important, some said, as when the first fish crawled from the sea on to land. The time was 2.56 A.M. GMT on July 21, 1969.

Armstrong began to move around on the Moon, gaining confidence with every step. He examined the landing gear of the lunar module and began to dig in the soil. Aldrin followed him down to the surface a quarter of an hour later. Together they surveyed the flat, dusty plain, scattered with angular rocks. 'Magnificent desolation,' commented Aldrin. They unveiled a plaque on one of the LM's legs. It read: 'Here men from the planet Earth first set foot upon the Moon, July 1969 A.D. We came in peace for all mankind'.

Armstrong and Aldrin walked on the Moon for over two hours, practising moving in the unfamiliar low gravity, collecting samples, and setting up experiments. All too soon, it seemed, the adventure had to end. Aldrin clambered back up the stairway into the lunar module, followed by Armstrong. Weary but satisfied, the two men repressurized the lunar module, took off their helmets and gloves, and quietly congratulated each other. For the first time, they noticed the smell of the Moon. To them it smelt like wet ashes or spent gunpowder caps from a toy pistol.

They ate and then settled down for seven hours' rest. Armstrong rigged a hammock across the small cabin while Aldrin curled up on the floor. They still had to face the critical moment of lift off from the Moon's surface. If the LM failed them then, they would be stranded on the Moon to die. But the Moon-bug proved reliable.

For seven minutes the ascent engine fired, speeding them to 6400 km/h. In orbit around the Moon again, Armstrong and Aldrin docked with the mother ship and transferred their priceless collection of Moon rocks in preparation for the trip home.

They returned on July 24 to a heroes' welcome. Even then, the ordeal was not over, for they and their cargo had to spend the next 18 days in quarantine lest some germ lurked among the lunar dust that might escape and harm life on Earth. But tests soon showed that the lunar soil was totally sterile. Quarantine procedures were eased for the next mission, and subsequently abandoned. Samples from other worlds such as Mars might yet prove to contain microscopic organisms, so the prospect of contamination from space remains a real fear for future explorers.

Apollo 11 was the fulfilment of President Kennedy's commitment. But it was more than that. For the first time, humans had reached out and touched another world. There was life on another body in space, albeit temporarily. Earth men had become Moon men, and even if they were not likely to become naturalized lunar citizens, the Earth was no longer the only place in space for humans to live. The footprints of those first explorers will remain visible in the dust of the airless, waterless Moon for millions of years – unless eradicated by careless tourists.

In the event, two Apollo missions landed on the Moon and returned before President Kennedy's deadline expired. Apollo 12's lunar module piloted by Pete Conrad and Alan Bean landed on November 19 in the Ocean of Storms, just a short walk away from the Surveyor 3 spacecraft which had landed automatically two and a half years before. Conrad and Bean snipped off parts of the Surveyor for later examination on Earth, where it was found that some terrestrial microorganisms

Apollo 12 astronauts Conrad and Bean set up this experimental device before collecting rock samples from the surface of the lifeless Moon. Tests have shown that lunar rocks contain useful amounts of metals such as iron, aluminium and titanium.

had clung to existence on the Surveyor even in the hostile lunar vacuum. Life was showing itself to be pretty tenacious.

Conrad and Bean spent 31½ hours on the lunar surface, 10 hours more than Armstrong and Aldrin. They performed two Moon walks, collecting a total of 34 kilograms of rocks, half as much again as the Apollo 11 crew. Already, exploring the Moon was starting to seem commonplace. Unlucky Apollo 13 in April 1970 showed that that was not the case.

On the third day in space as it approached the Moon, an oxygen tank in Apollo 13's service module exploded, causing widespread damage. In the command module astronauts Jim Lovell, John Swigert and Fred Haise heard a bang and felt the craft shake. They could see plumes of gas venting from one side of the service module, which put the spacecraft into a gentle spin. Warning lights flashed on, indicating loss of power from the electricity-generating fuel cells and of a steady leak from an oxygen tank. Mission control at Houston immediately cancelled the Moon landing and set about devising plans for the return of the astronauts, who faced death.

With their power and air supplies dwindling, the astronauts turned to the lunar module as a lifeboat. Using its engine and controls, they swung around behind the Moon and put themselves on course for an immediate return to Earth. The spacecraft became increasingly cold and stuffy. Condensation formed on the walls as temperatures fell to 3°C; it was like being trapped inside a refrigerator.

For the next three days the astronauts endured the cramped, uncomfortable conditions knowing that the shadow of death lay darkly over them. Fortunately, the lunar module proved equal to its unexpected task. It got them back to Earth. With a grateful farewell the astronauts jettisoned it and the buckled service module before they re-entered the atmosphere. As the g-forces built up during re-entry, droplets of condensation produced a rain shower inside the command module.

This real-life drama ended happily as Apollo 13's three orange-and-white parachutes blossomed to lower the command module gently into the Pacific Ocean. No one could know how close the crew of Apollo 13 had come to dying in space. Had the explosion occurred after the lunar module had been detached for the Moon landing, there seems little chance they could have survived. Learning from this accident, NASA engineers modified the service module to prevent such a potentially fatal failure occurring again.

The next flight saw the return to space of America's first astronaut, Alan Shepard, who had been grounded after his first flight because of an ear disorder, but following an operation in 1969 he was passed fit to fly again. Apollo 14 was an ambitious mission, involving exploration of a hilly region known as Fra Mauro. Touchdown on February 5, 1971 was a mere 27 metres from the target. Shepard and Edgar Mitchell made two extended Moonwalks totalling over 9 hours, including a 2.8 kilometre hike by Shepard to explore the blocky rim of an impact crater known as Cone crater.

The success of Apollo 14 restored NASA's confidence and set the stage for even greater adventures. Apollo 15 took to the Moon an electrically powered lunar car, stored folded in a spare compartment in the lunar module's lower stage. This wire-wheeled Moon car, with a top speed of 16 km/h, allowed astronauts to explore much wider areas of the Moon than on foot, keeping in direct touch with Earth via an umbrella-like aerial mounted on the vehicle. Next to the aerial was a colour TV camera which controllers on Earth steered by radio command to keep a constant eye on the astronauts' activities.

David Scott and James Irwin touched down on July 30, 1971 next to a lunar ravine called Hadley rille, within sight of the lunar Apennine mountains at the edge of the Mare Imbrium (Sea of Rains). Improved spacesuits and modifications to the lunar module allowed them to stay on the Moon for 67 hours. Among their activities during three EVAs the astronauts drove 27 kilometres on the Moon, collecting nearly 77 kilograms of samples, among them one particularly ancient rock which gave geologists additional clues to the formation and early history of the Moon.

One of the most worrisome of all space medical episodes occurred when both Scott and Irwin suffered heart irregularities as they transferred back into the command module after leaving the Moon. For Irwin, this turned out to be the start of a history of heart trouble. Charles Berry, NASA's leading space doctor, attributed the events to a lack of potassium in the astronauts' diets, corrected in subsequent flights.

By the middle of the next century it is probable that mines will have been established on the Moon and the extracted minerals processed in space. Since the Moon has a low gravity and no atmosphere to impede moving objects, material from the lunar mines could be 'catapulted' to the space processing station using a device known as a mass driver. Bags of lunar ore are loaded into containers and accelerated by magnetic forces along a track. When the containers reach lunar escape velocity (2.4 km/sec), the payload is ejected into space and caught in the net of the processing plant, while the containers return to be refilled. Manufacturing industries in space based on processed lunar materials would supply finished goods to Earth.

By now, the Apollo programme was drawing to a close, but the experience gained was being put to good use. Astronauts had demonstrated that they could move around happily and safely under the one-sixth gravity of the Moon despite the cumbersome inflated spacesuits that inevitably restricted their movements. The Moon's surface turned out to be firm enough to take the weight of men and lunar module; there were no deep dust drifts, crumbly lava fields or hidden crevasses as some astronomers had feared.

Landing sites that had initially been dismissed as too dangerous became targets for the later Apollo missions. Apollo 16 landed on April 21, 1972, in a jumbled highland region near the crater Descartes. Astronauts John Young and Charles Duke were in search of ancient lunar crust, but during their three-day stay all they found were rocks that had been hopelessly scrambled by aeons of impacts, making it impossible for geologists to tell what their original composition had been. While on the Moon, John Young was informed that plans were going ahead for the construction of the United States' next generation of spacecraft, the Space Shuttle. By a quirk of fate, it was Young himself who was to fly the first Shuttle into orbit.

The Apollo series ended with a blockbuster that set new records for the longest time spent on the Moon (75 hours), the longest single EVA (7½ hours), the maximum distance covered by the Moon car, 35 kilometres, and the heaviest load of lunar samples, 113 kilograms. The flight itself was the longest Apollo mission of all, lasting 12½ days from lift off to splashdown.

For the first time, an Apollo mission departed at night, the brilliant glare of the Saturn V's engines lighting up Cape Canaveral like a second Sun as Gene Cernan, Ronald Evans and Harrison ('Jack') Schmitt took off on December 7, 1972. Four days later Cernan and Schmitt landed their lunar module Challenger in a valley at the edge of the Sea of Serenity near the crater Littrow. On the horizon the brightness of the Taurus mountains contrasted with the dark, pulverized lava of the lowland plains on which they stood. Schmitt, a geologist, was in his element among the varied rocks.

The history of the Moon, as pieced together from the Apollo findings, starts 4600 million years ago when the Moon and Earth condensed out of a swirling cloud of dust surrounding the new-born Sun. A crust formed as the Moon cooled from the heat of its birth, but 4000 million years ago this crust was battered by swarms of debris left over from the formation of the planets. Molten lava oozed from the Moon's interior to fill the scars left by the impacting bodies, forming the dark lowland plains. About 2000 million years ago the lava from the Moon's interior dried up. Since then, very little has happened on the Moon, apart from the occasional impact which has dug a new large crater here and there, and a steady rain of micrometeorites which has broken up the lunar surface rocks to form a deep layer of densely compacted dust.

Apollo 17's Cernan and Schmitt left the Moon on December 14, 1972. Since then, no one has been to the Moon, nor are there plans for anyone to return in the foreseeable future.

It is the misfortune of historical events that their full importance is often recognized only in retrospect. Television viewers watching the exploration of the Moon were not always impressed by the entertainment value of history-as-it-happens. But the explorations of Apollo have subtly changed our outlook on ourselves and our world.

A total of 12 humans walked on the Moon over a period of 3½ years. During that time the people of planet Earth came to regard the Moon as an outpost of their own planet — remote and hostile, certainly, but no more alien than the Antarctic. In our generation, another body in space has become a place where suitably equipped humans can live and work. There are riches to be had there, too. Analysis of the Moon rocks shows them to contain plentiful raw materials for industry — metals such as aluminium, titanium and iron.

As life moves off our planet, the Moon will inevitably become a colony of Earth — and eventually a self-governing body. The success of project Apollo proved there is no barrier to the spread of life off Earth. How we capitalize on that is in the hands of the next human generation.

Chapter Three

STATIONS IN SPACE

For the last time, the thunder of a Saturn V rolled over the low scrub that binds the silver sands of Cape Canaveral to the Florida shoreline. On this occasion, May 14, 1973, there was not an Apollo spacecraft at the rocket's tip. Instead, the entire third stage had been converted into a space station, a combined scientific workshop and house in the sky for crews of three astronauts.

The workshop contained equipment for observing the Sun and Earth, and to study the effects of weightlessness on various materials as well as on the astronauts themselves. The space station was called Skylab. Its purpose was to demonstrate that humans could live and work productively in space for extended periods. As things turned out, the astronauts were put through a far greater test than anyone could have envisaged, for the entire mission was jeopardized by a freak accident during launch that required a daring repair job by the first crew.

Sixty–three seconds after the Saturn V bearing Skylab began to power its way into the sky that warm spring afternoon, air rushing past the rocket tore off an outer sheathing designed to protect the space station from the Sun's rays and impact by micrometeorites. As the sheathing was ripped away it took with it one of two wing-like solar panels intended to unfold in orbit to provide electricity; the other panel became jammed shut. Ground controllers realized the problem when Skylab in orbit 435 kilometres high

began overheating and was starved of electrical power. In that state Skylab was uninhabitable. With the whole project on the verge of ruins the launch of the first crew, planned for the following day, was cancelled while engineers sought answers to the problem.

In a startlingly short 10 days a solution had been devised, the equipment constructed and the astronauts had rehearsed rescue procedures in a water tank that simulated working in weightlessness. The plan was to deploy a sunshade to protect the station from the Sun's rays, and to cut free the jammed solar panel. On May 25 astronauts Pete Conrad, Joseph Kerwin and Paul Weitz took off in an Apollo capsule atop the smaller Saturn IB rocket. Aboard with them were a sunshade and a set of special cutting tools.

They soon hove to alongside the crippled space station. Skylab was basically a cylinder 25 metres long, varying in diameter from 3 metres to 6.7 metres. At the narrowest end was the docking adapter which contained two docking ports, one in line with the station and the second at right angles for an emergency rescue mission. The docking adapter housed control consoles for the Skylab solar telescope and experimental equipment including a furnace. Linking the docking adapter with the main Skylab workshop was an airlock section which could be depressurized for spacewalks.

Mounted outside the docking adapter was a battery of six telescopes for observing the Sun in a wide range of wavelengths. A windmill-like array of four solar panels provided power for this section; at first, it was the only source of power available to the damaged space station. The main body of Skylab consisted of the workshop section, which was divided into living quarters and an experiment area. Skylab's total habitable volume was 340 cubic metres, equivalent to that of a three-bedroom house.

Hovering alongside Skylab, Weitz leaned out of the command module's hatch in an attempt to pry free the jammed solar array, but without success.

For the time being they abandoned the attempt. After docking with Skylab the astronauts cautiously entered the space station, wearing masks in case the high temperatures had led to emission of toxic gases. Fortunately the atmosphere proved safe. Although the temperature inside Skylab was a scorching 55°C, low humidity made it bearable. Skylab used an atmosphere of one-quarter nitrogen, three-quarters oxygen at one-third atmospheric pressure.

The damaged Skylab; with incredible skill, astronauts erected the orange parasol to shade the craft before going outside to cut free the jammed solar panel.

The most pressing task was to protect the space station from the Sun's rays. To do this required using one of the small airlocks in the station's walls which were originally intended for mounting scientific experiments. The astronauts attached a box containing an umbrella-like sunshade to one of these airlocks. They gently pushed the sunshade out of the airlock until it snapped open. With a large area of Skylab's outer wall now shaded from the Sun, interior temperatures fell to a more Earth-like 30°C.

Some power was being supplied to the station by the solar observatory array, but not enough. Based on pictures televised back from the space station, ground teams worked out procedures for cutting the jammed solar wing free, and described these to the Skylab crew. On their twelfth day in the station, Conrad and Kerwin donned spacesuits and floated outside. In the following 3½ hours they were to perform the most difficult and dangerous task ever attempted in open space.

Conrad and Kerwin's spacesuits were supplied with air and cooling water from Skylab via an umbilical line which also acted as a tether to prevent the astronauts drifting off irretrievably into space. Those tethers proved vital. Using long-handled cutters, Conrad and Kerwin attempted to cut a metal strap that was holding the solar wing closed. As the strap was severed, Conrad tumbled off the space station, but the tether held him. To open the solar array fully he had to attach a rope and pull it. As the solar array suddenly swung open he lost balance again and went tumbling for a second time. Such daring exploits, never envisaged when the Skylab programme was planned, saved the space station. They underlined the value of man in space.

Working in weightlessness was proving easier than it had done on Gemini, a result both of the improved cooling of the spacesuits and of extensive underwater training. A further demonstration of running repairs occurred later in the mission when an electrical contact in the solar observatory stuck open, preventing power from reaching the observatory. Under instructions from the ground, Conrad went outside and struck the offending equipment a blow with a hammer – not very scientific, but it worked.

With the continued functioning of Skylab assured, the three-man crew could at last settle down to a normal routine aboard their space home.

A converted rocket casing may not sound a very appealing place in which to spend several weeks of your life. Living in a space station has certain similarities with being aboard a submarine – and indeed Skylab's designers used experience gained from long-duration submarine voyages in such matters as interior colouration, layout and lighting. One early decision of Skylab's designers was to retain the concept of floors and ceilings, to help weightless astronauts orient themselves in the cavernous interior of the space station – though in practice, orientation was seldom a problem.

'You do have a sense of up and down, and you can change it in two seconds whenever it's convenient,' reported scientist-astronaut Dr Joe Kerwin. 'If you go from one module into the other and you're upside down, you just say to your brain, "Brain, I want that way to be up." And your brain says, "Okay, then that way is up." And if you want to rotate 90 degrees and work that way, your brain will follow you.'

Pete Conrad was also enjoying the freedom of floating around in the workshop. 'Mobility around here is super,' he declared. 'Nobody has any motion sickness.' Later crews, though, did suffer from space motion sickness. Nearly all the astronauts found weightlessness to be fun, once they were used to it. Said scientist-astronaut Kerwin: 'It was a continuous and pleasant surprise to me to find out how easy it was to live in zero g, and how good we felt.' William Pogue of the third crew, though, would have preferred a station with gravity.

One of the more obvious adjustments to weightlessness was that the astronauts became about 2.5 centimetres taller, because the spine stretches in the absence of gravity. Their faces also became fatter and redder and their legs thinner as blood pooled in the upper parts of their bodies. These changes rapidly reversed when they returned to Earth. One embarrassing side-effect of life in space is increased flatulence. After his flight, Joe Kerwin reported: 'It is very difficult to belch. One does swallow a great deal of gas, and the gastrointestinal system processes it downward very effectively with great volume and frequency.'

Handrails and other restraints were provided liberally around Skylab for the crew to hold themselves in position when working. To stand upright in weightlessness the astronauts wore shoes with triangular plates on their soles which would lock into the triangular gridwork of the workshop's floor and ceiling.

Skylab's air-conditioning system proved to have an unexpected use. Loose objects found their way to the air filters and screens, so astronauts learned to look there first for missing items. One large screen became a favourite workbench, for tools and equipment stuck to it as though under gravity. Because of Skylab's low atmospheric pressure, sound did not travel well beyond a few feet, so astronauts talked to each other, and to ground control, via a dozen intercom stations situated throughout Skylab.

Dinner time aboard Skylab was a sumptuous affair compared with earlier space missions. To eat, crewmen gathered around a table which contained three food trays. They could have sat on a metal bar as a 'chair' but they usually preferred to stand – in weightlessness it really makes no difference. Each food tray had seven receptacles to hold cans; three of the receptacles had heaters for warming the food. The astronauts chose their own diet from a varied menu. Foods were eaten with a spoon or fork, magnetized to stick on the table. Skylab contained a refrigerator for frozen food, and ice cream was a favourite delicacy of the crews. Food tastes bland in space, probably a result of the excess of blood in the astronaut's head; later crews took more spices with them. Drinks were packaged in powdered form in plastic squeeze containers, and were prepared by injecting hot or cold water from outlets at the centre of the table.

All crewmembers had words of praise for the orbital toilet, located on a wall, which used a flow of air in place of gravity to separate wastes from the astronaut's body and deposit them in a collection bag. For defecation, the astronaut first inserted a collection bag into the commode, then strapped himself into place on the toilet seat with a belt across his lap. Foot restraints and handholds assisted the astronaut in holding himself firmly in position. The contents of the bag were afterwards heat dried and the bags were stored for return to Earth or dumped into the waste tank at one end of the station. Urine was collected in separate bags either through a collector located just below the toilet seat or by a separate funnel which could be used when standing. Urine samples were frozen for later analysis on Earth.

For the first time in space, astronauts were able to take a shower. The astronaut pulled up a cylindrical shower curtain around him and squirted himself with water from a handheld spray which was fed from a pressurized water container. Airflow did the job of gravity in drawing the water to the bottom of the shower, although crewmen complained that the shower took a long time to dry out afterwards. Paul Weitz, first to use the shower, reported: 'It took a fair amount longer to use than you might expect, but you come out smelling good.' For normal hand washing, a small water spray in a vacuum sink sufficed.

Towels, wet wipes and tissues were provided, along with a vacuum cleaner for sucking up floating debris. Each crewman had his own personal hygiene kit containing a toothbrush, toothpaste, comb, nail clippers, deodorant, hand cream, shaving cream, and a choice of electric or blade razors. Inside Skylab astronauts wore casual clothes, including gold-coloured shirts, trousers and jackets made of fire-resistant material. Bending down to put on socks and shoes proved to be an effort in weightlessness; astronauts came back with strengthened stomach muscles.

For recreation the crew were provided with books, playing cards, darts with Velcro tips, exercise equipment and taped music. One of the favourite pastimes turned out to be gazing at the Earth below or at the stars at night. To sleep, each crewman retired to his own curtained-off area. Beds are unnecessary in weightlessness; instead, the astronauts zip-

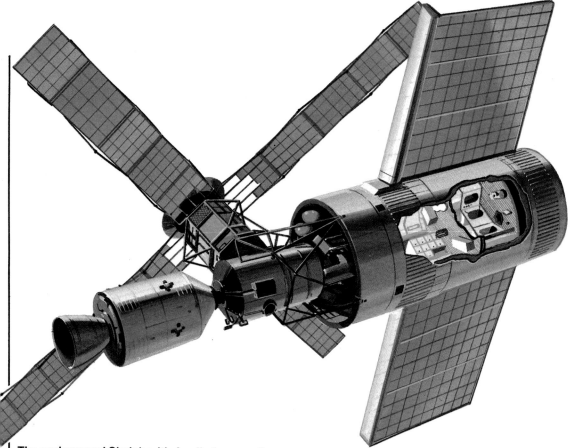

The undamaged Skylab with Apollo ferry craft attached. Its huge solar panels provided power for the workshop, living quarters and telescopes.

ped themselves up in sleeping bags hung from the wall. All Skylab astronauts slept well. One unexpected difficulty in the sleep compartments was in reaching out in the dark to touch the light switch a mere 60 centimetres away. Said Owen Garriott, scientist-astronaut on the second Skylab crew: 'The result was not just a near miss. We found that our hands might encounter a locker as much as 45 degrees away from the correct direction. Although I tried to practice this move on a number of occasions, I still could not do it well after two months.' In weightlessness, visual cues are vital for coordination.

Once they had completed their repair of the crippled space station, the first crew carried out a full programme of scientific experiments and observations. One of the main experimental programmes utilized the array of six telescopes at Skylab's side to observe the Sun in ultraviolet light and X-rays which do not penetrate the atmosphere and are therefore unobservable from Earth. Such observations have told astronomers more about the violent storms and eruptions that occur on the Sun, and provide clues to ways in which the activity may affect climate on Earth.

The Earth itself was another important object of study. Cameras and instruments such as radar were used to study vegetation, soil, geological formations, ocean currents, and weather systems. Skylab's orbit covered three-quarters of the Earth's surface, from 50 degrees north to 50 degrees south, passing over the same area every 5 days.

A third area of investigation was production of new materials in weightlessness. Without the effect of gravity, fluids of different density can be made to mix that do not blend on Earth, allowing the production of new alloys and glasses. In addition, much

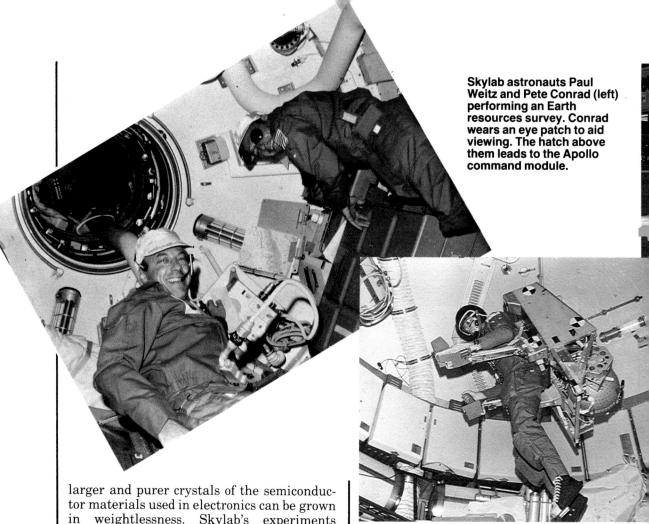

Skylab astronauts Paul Weitz and Pete Conrad (left) performing an Earth resources survey. Conrad wears an eye patch to aid viewing. The hatch above them leads to the Apollo command module.

larger and purer crystals of the semiconductor materials used in electronics can be grown in weightlessness. Skylab's experiments opened the way to orbital factories, producing new metals and electronic components for sale on Earth.

After 28 days in space, longer than any humans before them, the first Skylab crew returned to Earth on June 22, 1973, bringing with them the results of their experiments, plus the certain knowledge that humans can perform effectively in space. Five weeks later, they were replaced by a second crew – Alan Bean, Owen Garriott and Jack Lousma – who took off from Cape Canaveral on July 28 for an intended 56-day stay.

But soon came a worrying failure in the Apollo service module, which threatened the mission. Two of the four small jet clusters on the side of the service module used for steering the Apollo stopped working. Loss of these thruster units could have endangered the

astronauts' safe return to Earth, so ground controllers put in motion plans for a rescue mission. An Apollo command module had been modified for this eventuality. The rescue Apollo would be launched with two men aboard and return to Earth with five, two of them on emergency couches squeezed underneath the three normal Apollo seats. Fortunately, no rescue was needed. Ground controllers ruled that the Apollo could return safely with its two remaining sets of thrusters, which Lousma and Garriott inspected during a spacewalk and found to be in full working order.

Shortly after reaching orbit, first Lousma and then Bean and Garriott suffered space sickness. Lousma actually vomited up his evening meal. They were slowed by this sickness for the first few days, but by August 6 all

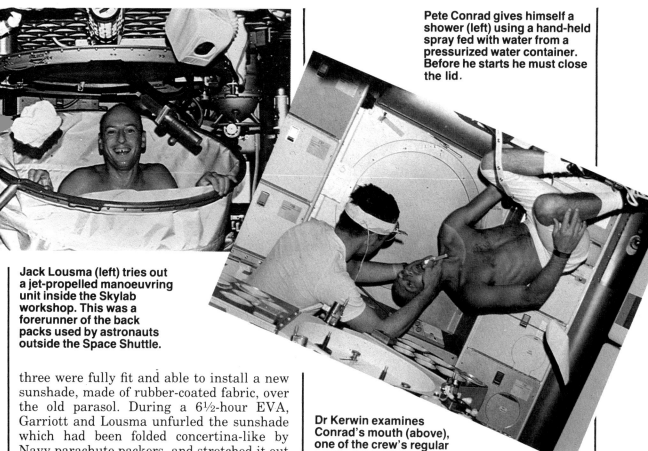

Jack Lousma (left) tries out a jet-propelled manoeuvring unit inside the Skylab workshop. This was a forerunner of the back packs used by astronauts outside the Space Shuttle.

Dr Kerwin examines Conrad's mouth (above), one of the crew's regular medical experiments.

three were fully fit and able to install a new sunshade, made of rubber-coated fabric, over the old parasol. During a 6½-hour EVA, Garriott and Lousma unfurled the sunshade which had been folded concertina-like by Navy parachute packers, and stretched it out over an A-shaped frame made from sections of aluminium pole. On this same EVA they loaded new film into the solar observatory's telescopes.

Settled into their new home in space, Bean and his crew found it easy to work long hours without fatigue. So efficient did they become in carrying out their tasks that they repeatedly asked for more to do. They completed a haul of over 14,000 photographs of the Earth and 29 kilometres of taped data. They spent 305 hours observing the Sun, 100 hours longer than scheduled, leading to a bonanza of 77,000 photographs of the Sun.

Among the experiments taken into orbit by the second Skylab crew were a number suggested by American high-school children, including the famous space spiders Arabella and Anita. Observation of the web-spinning ability of a spider in a transparent plastic frame was a simple and fascinating way of determining how quickly an organism can adapt to weightlessness. Arabella at first span tangled webs, but after a few attempts she was spinning webs similar to those on Earth, with the interesting difference that the thread was thinner than under Earth's gravity. Anita, by the time it was her turn to perform, had adapted sufficiently to spin normal webs. Other experiments with minnows showed that fish brought from Earth at first swam in tight loops under weightlessness, but those which hatched from eggs aboard Skylab swam normally from the start.

Within the confines of the workshop area, Bean and his crew tried out prototype jet-propelled backpacks. Improved versions will be used by astronauts outside the Space Shuttle, to inspect satellites or participate in the building of large structures in space.

Following the success of the second Skylab crew, the third and final Skylab visit was extended to 84 days. On November 16, 1973, a Saturn IB rocket took off from Cape Canaveral carrying Gerald Carr, Ed Gibson and William Pogue, none of whom had flown in space before. This crew noted that there is a definite adjustment period during the first few days in orbit, which they compared with the period of acclimatization needed when moving from sea level to a high altitude, only much more pronounced.

Pogue was a member of the U.S. Air Force aerobatic team, the Thunderbirds, and was not at all susceptible to motion sickness on Earth. Ironically, once in space he became almost immediately ill; that night, he vomited. Medicines eased the problem, and in a few days he was feeling fine again.

Most Skylab astronauts adapted to weightlessness in three to four days, and after a week none had any symptoms of space sickness. Remarkably enough, once adapted to weightlessness they seemed to achieve immunity to motion sickness. In tests on Earth, astronauts were spun on a chair rotating at 10 to 20 revolutions per minute while moving their heads from side to side. After 50 to 70 head movements they began to feel queasy. But in space they performed up to 150 head movements spinning at 30 revs per minute without experiencing symptoms of sickness. Their sensitivity to motion sickness returned to normal after approximately two weeks back on Earth. Because the mission gave each of the astronauts more time in space than anyone before them, emphasis was placed on medical studies.

Space doctors knew from previous flights that astronauts returned with a smaller volume of blood, lower body weight and reduced efficiency of blood circulation as a result of exposure to weightlessness. But it took the extended Skylab missions to show that these changes do not continue indefinitely. Loss of weight by astronauts early in their flights is explained by two factors: reduction in volume of body fluid and a shrinking of muscles, particularly leg muscles. An astronaut's body interprets the upward shift of blood in weightlessness as being due to an overall excess of body fluids. The astronaut's body responds so that he excretes more water through urination and drinks less. Another response is that the body makes fewer new red blood cells. After a few weeks astronauts cease to lose blood volume or muscle tissue, and by the end of the third Skylab mission the crew's body weight had started to return to normal.

Many of the effects of weightlessness are similar to those observed in people who have been confined to bed for periods of months. Not surprisingly, therefore, the best way to counteract the effects of weightlessness is through exercise. Each day the astronauts spent some time pedalling on an exercise bicycle; the third crew also walked on a treadmill. Exercise time each day was increased from half an hour for the first crew to one hour for the second crew and ultimately one-and-a-half hours per day for the final crew.

Every three to four days the astronaut tested himself in the so-called Lower Body Negative Pressure device. This was a cylinder in which the astronaut was sealed up to the waist while air was pumped out to create a pressure difference between the top and bottom halves of the astronaut's body, simulating the strain placed on the blood circulation system by standing upright under Earth's gravity. In some tests, mostly in the first few weeks of the missions, the astronauts came close to fainting (anyone who has stood up suddenly after lying down will have experienced similar sensations). Results from the pressure cylinder experiments showed that, in common with the blood volume and body weight, the astronauts' circulatory systems adapted to weightlessness and stabilized after five to seven weeks. Once back on the ground all the Skylab astronauts rapidly readjusted to Earth's gravity, the recovery being quickest for those who had undertaken more exercise while in orbit.

One significant body change which had not levelled off by the end of the last Skylab mission was loss of calcium from the astronauts' bones. After three months in space the third Skylab crew had lost an average of two per cent of their total body calcium. In itself this amount of loss is not dangerous, but the

A spell in the Lower Body Negative Pressure Device every few days allowed the astronauts' cardio-vascular systems to be monitored.

losses seem to come mostly from load-bearing bones. If losses continued at this rate, American space doctors predicted that astronauts would return to Earth with dangerously brittle bones after a year or so in space unless effective countermeasures were developed.

The third and final Skylab crew returned to Earth on February 8, 1974. The giant space station had been manned for a total of 171 days, during which the three crews orbited the Earth nearly 2500 times, covering over 113 million kilometres in all. A total of 42 hours were spent outside the space station in EVA. The astronauts took over 180,000 photographs of the Sun and 40,000 of the Earth. Abandoned in orbit, Skylab took its final bow in June 1979 when it crashed to Earth, scattering red-hot fragments over the Australian outback.

Humans have survived, and even thrived, in space for longer periods than the Skylab astronauts in a series of Soviet space stations called Salyut. These extended flights, though, got off to a bad start.

Salyut 1 was launched in April 1971, two years before the American Skylab. Salyut 1's first crew, Georgi Dobrovolsky, Viktor Patsayev and Vladislav Volkov, arrived in a Soyuz craft for a stay of 23 days, then a record.

Salyut was shaped like three interconnecting cylinders, the widest being 4.1 metres across. Overall it was 13 metres long and weighed approximately 19 tonnes. Its internal volume was 99 cubic metres, about a quarter that of Skylab. Salyut's interior was designed with a much stronger sense of horizontal and vertical than in Skylab. Salyut's floor (actually, one long side of the cylinder) was painted a darker colour than the walls and ceiling to give a psychological effect of up and down.

Salyut 1's three-man crew carried out work similar to that later to be done aboard Skylab. They exercised for a total of two hours a day using a treadmill device; later Salyuts included an exercise bicycle. For much of the time the Salyut cosmonauts wore elasticated 'penguin' suits which subjected their bodies to a strain to compensate for the absence of gravity. The 'penguin' name comes from the waddling motion cosmonauts made when trying it out on Earth. Later flights included tests with a suit that subjected the lower half of the cosmonaut's body to reduced pressure, similar to the Lower Body Negative Pressure cylinder on Skylab.

The cosmonauts ate a variety of canned meats, plus cheese and yoghurt preserved in an on-board refrigerator. Salyut had a toilet similar to Skylab's. The cosmonauts washed themselves with damp towels, cleaned their teeth with edible chewing gum and shaved with normal safety razors and shaving foam.

All seemed to have gone well. On June 29, 1971, Dobrovolsky, Patsayev and Volkov loaded up their Soyuz with the results of their experiments and took their seats for the return to Earth. After undocking they jettisoned the spherical orbital module of Soyuz, but at that stage all communications with the craft ceased. The Soyuz landed automatically. When the recovery crews reached the craft, they found all three cosmonauts dead in their seats.

For the second time, Soyuz flights were suspended while the craft was redesigned. In this case, it seemed that a valve had stuck open when the orbital compartment was jettisoned; the Soyuz rapidly depressurized, killing the crew. Spacesuits would have saved them, had they been wearing any, but Soyuz was not roomy enough to accommodate a crew of three in spacesuits. Following this accident, Soyuz crews were reduced to two men only, each wearing a spacesuit.

Salyut 1 re-entered the Earth's atmosphere in October 1971. It was replaced in April 1973 by Salyut 2, but this broke up in orbit. Not until July 1974 did the Soviet Union complete its first successful mission to a space station, when Pavel Popovich and Yuri Artyukhin spent 14 days aboard Salyut 3. By then, of course, the Skylab astronauts had set far more impressive records.

Bad luck continued to dog the Soviet space programme. There were docking failures and even a Soyuz launch abort before Pyotr Klimuk and Vitaly Sevastyanov completed a 64-day mission in 1975 aboard Salyut 4 – not as long as the third Skylab crew but still impressive. To the discomfort of Klimuk and Sevastyanov, excess humidity in the Salyut fogged the space station's windows and led to the build-up of green mold on the inner walls.

In preparation for their return to Earth, Soviet space doctors had instructed them to exercise more during the last ten days of the flight and to increase their intake of water and salt, both of which are excreted by the body in weightlessness in an attempt to reduce blood volume. On landing, both cosmonauts left the capsule unaided. The day after landing they went swimming, jogged, and played tennis, to the doctors' surprise.

Virtually all spacemen have lost a few per cent of their body weight during their missions, a result of reduced blood volume and muscle mass in zero gravity. Sevastyanov lost 2 kilograms, but had regained it the day after

Soyuz spacecraft docked with a Salyut space station. The Soyuz with its spherical orbital module is on the left and the cylindrical Salyut with two cosmonauts at work is on the right. Salyut obtains its power from three solar panels.

Astronauts from the one and only joint US/USSR space mission toast each other with tubes of spacefood, wishfully relabelled 'vodka'.

landing, quicker than any previous cosmonaut, confirming the effectiveness of the medical procedures to combat the effects of weightlessness.

Bigger advances followed the launch in September 1977 of Salyut 6, an improved design which allowed a Soyuz to dock at each end. An unmanned tanker version of Soyuz, called Progress, was developed for automatic supply of the station. A succession of space endurance records lasting 96 days, 140 days, 175 days and 185 days were established in Salyut 6. Crews on these marathon flights were visited by cosmonauts who dropped in for a week at a time via the second docking port on Salyut. As part of an agreement with other Warsaw pact countries, visitors to Salyut 6 included cosmonauts from Czechoslovakia, Poland, East Germany, Bulgaria, Hungary, Vietnam, Cuba, Mongolia and Romania. The purpose of these international visits was as much political as it was scientific.

Yuri Romanenko and Georgi Grechko were the first Soviet cosmonauts to break the 84-day Skylab record, returning to Earth on March 16, 1978, after 96 days in space. Both were very tired and weak on landing, for they had done far less exercise in flight than doctors had ordered. They had to be carried from their spacecraft on stretchers. For the first few days back on Earth they found walking an effort; even to lift a cup of tea was a strain. After the freedom of weightlessness their beds seemed very hard, and they still tried to swim out of bed in the morning as they had done in Salyut. 'They are both still up there in space, not only physically but also mentally,' said space doctor Robert Dyakonov.

To help them readjust, for 12 days Romanenko and Grechko wore special inflatable trousers which placed pressure on the legs, preventing too much blood flowing into them under the pull of gravity. Similar devices had also been worn by the Skylab crewmen. Soviet space doctors predicted that, with suitable exercise, humans could live and work in space for a year or longer.

Further demonstration of this confidence about long-duration missions came on June

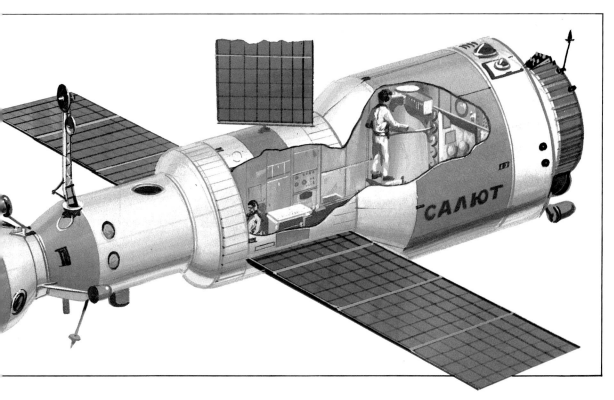

15, 1978, when Vladimir Kovalyonok and Alexander Ivanchenkov took off for what turned out to be a new record of 140 days in Salyut 6. On their return, doctors declared them to be in better condition than the 96-day cosmonauts.

The most remarkable story of the whole Salyut 6 programme concerns cosmonaut Valery Ryumin, who spent 175 days in the space station with Vladimir Lyakhov from February to August 1979. Seven months later he was back again in Salyut 6, this time with Leonid Popov, for 185 days. The reason was that the cosmonaut scheduled to fly with Popov was injured in training. Ryumin volunteered to take his place, and was accepted. Hence, between February 1979 and October 1980 he came to spend a staggering total of 12 months in space, making him by far the world's most experienced spaceman. How he tolerated living for so long in a volume no larger than one carriage of a London underground train remains a source of amazement.

Exercise on these missions was stepped up to more than two hours a day, with the cosmonauts walking and jogging 8 to 10 kilometres a day on their treadmill. They wore improved versions of the elasticated Penguin suit for 10 hours or more each day. Ryumin's weight on landing after the 175-day mission was the same as when he took off. During the subsequent 185-day mission he and Popov made space medical history by actually gaining weight – at one stage of the flight Ryumin, who put on 4.7 kilograms, reported that he was having to loosen his belt. Ryumin also surprised doctors by walking unaided from the capsule after this longest flight.

It seems therefore that many of the problems of weightlessness are now understood and can be combated by proper medical attention. Even the insidious loss of bone calcium had levelled off by the end of the longest flight. But there is a remaining problem. Follow-up studies on the Skylab astronauts found that their bones had still not returned to normal five years after their flights. This finding, if confirmed by Soviet data, may place a limit on the total time each human can safely spend in weightlessness.

What's the purpose of the long-duration Soviet sojourns in space? Their goal is to set up permanently inhabited bases in orbit around the Earth, with crews being replaced every few months. The Soviet Union is believed to be developing a space station, capable of housing up to 12 people, consisting of a central core to which additional modules can be plugged in. Such a station may well be set up by the end of the 1980s. Another stated objective is a flight to Mars, which would take a year or longer. On return from his marathon flight, Valery Ryumin said: 'If it was needed to prove we could go to Mars then Leonid Popov and I would volunteer right now.'

A Mars mission would be so difficult and so expensive that it's tempting to speculate that Russia and America would join forces on the expedition. There is a precedent. The first (and so far only) East-West space mission occurred in July 1975 when an American Apollo crewed by Tom Stafford, Vance Brand and Deke Slayton linked up in orbit with a Soviet Soyuz containing Alexei Leonov and Valery Kubasov. In the spirit of East-West detente which prevailed at the time, Soviet and American space officials spent three years planning the flight, which involved Apollo carrying a docking tunnel to link the two craft. The mission was jointly directed from Soviet and American space centres. Controllers and astronauts on both sides learned each other's language. During the flight, the spacemen moved between craft, conducting joint experiments. No further joint missions are planned. But it is possible that an American Space Shuttle may one day link up with a Soviet space station.

A manned flight to Mars would probably consist of two spacecraft, each carrying perhaps six people. Logically the effort should be divided, one craft being sponsored by western nations (the United States and Europe, possibly with Japanese involvement), while the other would be the product of the Soviet bloc. It would indeed be satisfying if the first manned trip to Mars were made by representatives of many nations on the planet Earth.

Chapter Four

THE UNIVERSE AROUND US

So far, astronauts have done no more than dip their toes into the vast ocean of space. Unmanned probes have ventured into deeper waters between the planets, but beyond the rim of the solar system is a gulf that separates us from the stars. Our fastest space probes would take 100,000 years to reach the nearest star to the Sun, fifty times longer than it would take to reach Mars at walking pace. The sheer volume of space means that much about the Universe may remain both unknown and unknowable.

Yet the limitless size of the Universe means that its possibilities are equally limitless. So it is difficult to resist the assumption that there must be other forms of life out there, possibly engaged in space exploration. If they are out there, it seems inevitable that one day we must meet them, or at least discover some unequivocal evidence of their existence, such as an incoming radio message. Let us survey the Universe and its contents to see the ways in which the Universe appears to be almost purpose-made for life.

First, some definitions. A planet is a body that does not shine of its own accord; it can be made of rock, metal or gas. Our Earth is one of nine planets orbiting a star called the Sun. In order of average distance from the Sun, the planets are: Mercury, Venus, Earth, Mars, Jupiter, Saturn, Uranus, Neptune and Pluto.

A star is a ball of gas that gives out its own light and heat. Stars form vast aggregations known as galaxies.

Every star in the sky is a sun, similar in nature to our own Sun. Some stars are bigger and brighter than the Sun, others smaller and cooler. But astronomers have found that our Sun seems to be a run-of-the-mill star, typical of what the Universe has to offer. That being so, the Earth and the life on it may also be typical products of nature.

All the stars visible to the naked eye on a clear night are members of a vast Catherine-wheel shaped spiral known as the Galaxy (given a capital letter to distinguish it from any other galaxy). Our Sun is one of at least 100,000 million stars in the Galaxy. Even if only a small fraction of those stars are similar to the Sun, and even if only a small percentage of those Sun-like stars have planets, that still leaves a large number of potential homes for life off Earth.

Most of the stars in the Galaxy seem to mass into a hazy band of light running across the sky, known as the Milky Way. The name Milky Way is popularly given to the entire Galaxy.

Distances in space are so immense that astronomers have invented their own measurements to supplant puny miles and kilometres. Most commonly used is the light

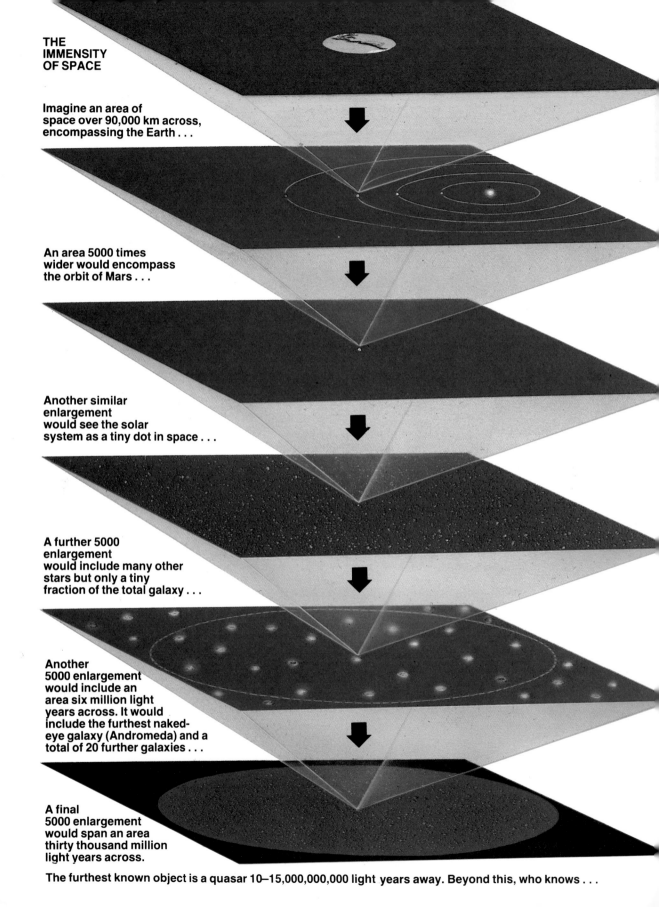

THE IMMENSITY OF SPACE

Imagine an area of space over 90,000 km across, encompassing the Earth . . .

An area 5000 times wider would encompass the orbit of Mars . . .

Another similar enlargement would see the solar system as a tiny dot in space . . .

A further 5000 enlargement would include many other stars but only a tiny fraction of the total galaxy . . .

Another 5000 enlargement would include an area six million light years across. It would include the furthest naked-eye galaxy (Andromeda) and a total of 20 further galaxies . . .

A final 5000 enlargement would span an area thirty thousand million light years across.

The furthest known object is a quasar 10–15,000,000,000 light years away. Beyond this, who knows . . .

There are three main types of galaxy: elliptical (left) containing mostly older stars; spiral (centre) similar to our own Milky Way; and barred spiral which has a bright central bar of stars and gas.

year, the distance across which a beam of light flashes in one year; it is equivalent to 5.9 million million miles (9.5 million million kilometres). The nearest star to the Sun, Alpha Centauri (actually a triplet of three stars linked by gravity, but appearing as one to the naked eye) is 4.3 light years away; this is typical of distances which separate stars in the Galaxy.

Until early this century it was assumed that the Sun lay somewhere near the centre of the Galaxy, but this fond notion was shattered in 1918 by an American astronomer, Harlow Shapley. He found that the Sun lay in the galactic suburbs, in a spiral arm about two thirds of the way to the Galaxy's edge.

Shapley's discovery still left open the question of what, if anything, lay beyond the edge of our Milky Way Galaxy. Some people believed that there was nothing else to be found in the Universe except empty space. But other astronomers had their suspicions about certain fuzzy, spiral-shaped objects known as spiral nebulae ('nebula' is the Latin for cloud). Perhaps these were separate galaxies of stars, too far away for us then to see.

The question was settled by the Mount Wilson 2.5 metre reflecting telescope, the largest in the world when it was opened in

1917. Sitting in the clear air of the evergreen-forested San Gabriel mountains outside Los Angeles at an altitude of 1740 metres, this giant eye could see farther into space than any instrument before. In the course of six years it was to create a double revolution in the hands of the American astronomer Edwin Hubble.

Repeatedly Hubble photographed the spiral nebulae with ever-better photographic emulsions until he found what he was looking for – individual stars whose brightness he could use to calibrate the nebulae's distance. In 1923 he discerned individual stars in the great spiral nebula in Andromeda, an object so large and bright it can be seen with the naked eye as a hazy patch on clear, dark nights. Modern photographs show it to be a swirling galaxy of stars, a twin of our own Milky Way Galaxy. The Andromeda galaxy is the farthest object visible to the naked eye, lying 2.2 million light years away – the light from it entering our eyes today started out 2.2 million years ago while our Australopithecine ancestors roamed the plains of Africa.

Hubble had established that other galaxies exist beyond our own – islands in space containing millions of stars and possibly life, though so unimaginably far away it would be

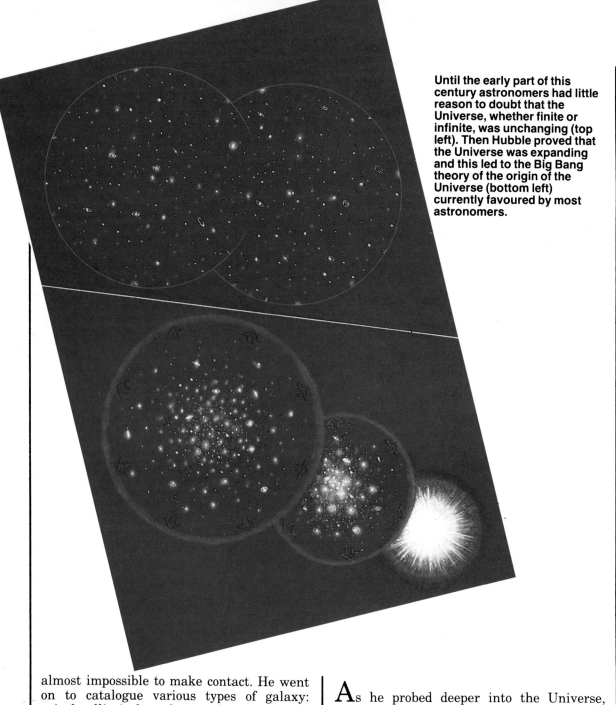

Until the early part of this century astronomers had little reason to doubt that the Universe, whether finite or infinite, was unchanging (top left). Then Hubble proved that the Universe was expanding and this led to the Big Bang theory of the origin of the Universe (bottom left) currently favoured by most astronomers.

almost impossible to make contact. He went on to catalogue various types of galaxy: spiral, elliptical, and irregular – categories which astronomers still use today. Peering into deepest space, our modern telescopes have revealed as many galaxies in the Universe as there are stars in our own Milky Way. Somewhere out there, there may be an almost-identical Earth with almost-identical humans. But we may never know for sure.

As he probed deeper into the Universe, Hubble uncovered a remarkable fact: the galaxies were moving. Not in random directions were they moving, but always outwards from the Milky Way, as though some cosmic force of repulsion were at work. Just looking at a galaxy is not enough to see it moving; what revealed the effect was analysis of the galaxies' light. If an object is moving away from us, light from it is stretched out in wavelength. A similar effect happens with sound: a receding bell or siren becomes deeper in tone, because its sound waves are stretched out. Lengthening of light waves is known as a red shift, because the light is shifted towards the red (long-wave) end of the spectrum. Hubble found that not only was the light from distant galaxies red shifted, a sure sign of their movement away from us, but that the amount of red shift increased with the galaxy's distance. In other words, the farther away a galaxy is from us, the faster it is moving.

Thanks to Hubble's law, as the relationship is called, astronomers can now estimate the distance to a remote galaxy by measuring the amount of its red shift. The most distant objects known in the Universe, called quasars, lie at distances of 10,000 million light years or more, according to their red shifts. Quasars are believed to be galaxies with very bright centres. They are so far away that we see them as they appeared long before our own Sun and Earth were born, early in the history of the Universe. By looking far off into space, therefore, we are also looking back in time. In that sense, telescopes are time machines.

Since the entire Universe appears to be expanding, it is natural to assume that in the past the Universe was smaller than it is now. Indeed, if we mentally reverse the expansion we realize that the Universe must once have been concentrated into a super-dense blob. For unknown reasons, that blob exploded. The galaxies are the bits from the explosion, still flying outwards as the space between them expands. That explosion, known as the Big Bang, marks the origin of the Universe as we know it. From current measurements of the rate of expansion of the Universe, astronomers estimate that the Big Bang occurred between 10,000 million and 20,000 million years ago. However, this simple picture of the Universe may well have to be modified in the light of future discoveries.

As for life off Earth, our own Milky Way Galaxy gives us scope enough for speculation without worrying about all those other galaxies. The key to life in the Universe is the stars. Not only do they provide the energy source for life, they have also produced the atoms of which living things are made. To see how this comes about, we must look at the life story of a star.

In the beginning, shortly after the Big Bang, the Universe consisted largely of hydrogen, the simplest substance in the Universe. Mixed in with every eleven hydrogen atoms was one helium atom, formed in the Big Bang inferno. The very first stars were made purely of this simple mixture, and indeed the overall composition of the Universe has changed very little since then. There are now slight impurities present in the Universe, amounting to about one atom in a thousand. For most purposes, this slight contamination might be thought of as trivial – except that our planet, and our bodies, are made of these impurities, excreted by the stars themselves.

Stars are born from great clouds of gas which collapse inwards under their own gravity. At the centre of a collapsing cloud of gas, as in the middle of a contracting crowd of people, temperatures and pressures increase. The ball of gas that will become a star begins to glow cherry red with heat released by its contraction. Eventually, conditions at the centre become so extreme that nuclear reactions switch on, tapping a source of power that turns the gas blob into a true star, emitting copious amounts of heat and light.

The bigger and brighter a star is, the quicker it burns out. The biggest stars of all – those 50 or so times as massive as the Sun – consume most of their fuel in a million years or less. In the early days of the Galaxy, 10 billion or more years ago, there must have been many such massive stars. When a massive star nears the end of its life it enters into a series of runaway nuclear reactions at its core which lead to the star splitting asunder in a nuclear holocaust. Such a cataclysmic stellar explosion is known as a supernova. A star that becomes a supernova temporarily emits as much energy as a billion Suns.

All the chemical elements of nature are forged in the nuclear blast furnace of a supernova. The star's innards are disgorged into space by the explosion where they mix with

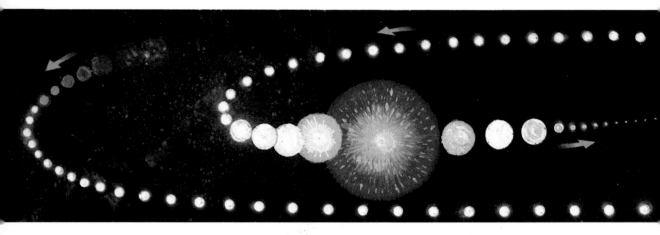

the existing clouds of hydrogen and helium gas. Subsequently these gas clouds, laced with their sprinkling of impurities, are collected up and formed into new stars, planets and, maybe, life.

The importance of supernovae in shaping the Universe cannot be overemphasized. Without past supernovae, we would not exist, and neither would the Earth. The very atoms of our bodies have been processed through nuclear reactions within generations of stars which lived and died before the Sun was born. We are all very old. The atoms of which we are made came into being 5,000 million years or more ago. They have been recycled through many bodies before reaching ours, and they will form part of the generations that come after us – generations that will carry our atoms back into space.

Our Sun will not suffer such a spectacular fate as a supernova. At present, the Sun is in stable middle age, drawing on stocks of hydrogen fuel at its centre as it has done for the past 4,700 million years. In a few billion years' time, though, the central hydrogen store will be used up, having been converted into helium by the nuclear fires. Eventually, the helium also joins in the energy-generating reactions, being turned into carbon.

By that stage, the Sun will have swelled up into a red giant star perhaps a hundred times its present diameter, large enough to engulf the orbit of the Earth. As the Sun swells, all life remaining on our planet will be roasted; the rest will have fled.

At its largest, the red giant Sun will become unstable. Its outer layers will drift off into space, forming a stellar smoke ring. Astronomers can see a number of these wreaths encircling the graves of stars formerly like the Sun. Among the material puffed off into space will be carbon produced inside the star – and carbon is the chemical backbone of life on Earth, because of its useful habit of linking up with many other atoms to form complex chains. So the relatively quiescent death of stars like the Sun is another way in which the atoms of life are distributed into space from the crucible of a stellar interior.

The gas clouds of space are like huge chemical laboratories in which atoms enter into a wide variety of liaisons, most of them based on carbon, the most gregarious atom of all; hydrogen, nitrogen and oxygen also feature prominently in the chemical combinations. These four atoms are the most important to life as we know it.

Astronomers observing at optical and radio wavelengths have detected over 50 different molecules out there whose tongue-twisting names attest to their chemical complexity. One, blessed with the laborious title of cyano-deca-penta-yne, contains 13 atoms, and there are likely to be yet more complex combinations awaiting discovery, perhaps including amino acids, the structural units of protein.

By itself, the existence of complex molecules based on carbon proves nothing about the existence of life off Earth; they are merely

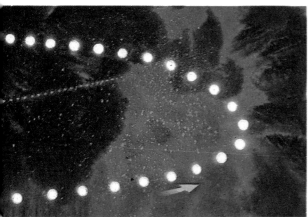

The life story of a star like the Sun (left). Born from clouds of gas in space the star evolves to stable middle age, then expands to become a red giant and finally fades into obscurity as a white dwarf.

Examples of the various stages in this life cycle of stars (below). The Orion nebula (1) is a gas cloud in which stars are forming. The Pleiades (2) are a cluster of young stars. The Ring nebula in Lyra (3) marks the death of a once glorious red giant.

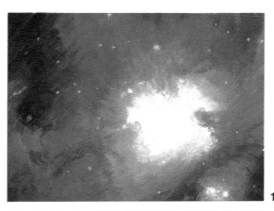

1

2

the building blocks of life, as far removed from a living cell as a pile of bricks is from a finished house. What's important is that the essentials of life are sprinkled liberally throughout the Galaxy, and they are concentrated in the very areas in which stars are born. Stars, it seems, come into being surrounded by a rich chemical fog containing the right ingredients for life.

Gas clouds in the Galaxy are so voluminous that each can spawn a whole cluster of stars, as is happening today in the nebula which marks the sword of the constellation Orion. The Orion nebula glows from the light of new-born stars at its centre, but there is enough surplus matter there to produce hundreds of stars yet. Once star formation is complete in the Orion nebula the area will probably look like the Pleiades, a young cluster of 200 or more stars in the constellation Taurus.

Our own Sun probably arose as one member of a cluster like the Pleiades, but the other stars have since dispersed, as is expected will happen to the Pleiades. Some members of a cluster are born so close together that they do not drift apart, but remain attached by each other's gravity to form a twin star or binary system. In some cases, more than two stars are linked in this way to form families of three, four or even six stars.

So much for stars. What about planets? During its birth a star is cocooned in gas and dust. This superfluous material may form into another, smaller star, or it may become

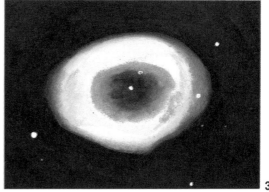

3

the assembly yard for a planetary system, as happened around our Sun. Gradually specks of dust will collide and build up into larger bodies until, after millions of years, the bodies have grown large enough to attract one another by gravity, thereby coalescing into planet-sized masses. This sweeping-up process continues until all the material is used up, or the cloud is blown away when the young star flares into life. Thus, planetary systems should be abundant, a natural by-product of the formation of stars. Moreover, those planets will be enveloped in gases rich in life-giving chemicals.

Firm evidence that our Sun was enveloped in such a chemical stew has come from meteorites, lumps of rock left over from the formation of the solar system which occasionally crash to Earth. Analysis of meteorites has shown that many of them contain organic molecules even more complex than those found in interstellar clouds, including amino acids, the building blocks of protein. These chemicals can only have been produced from the gas cloud surrounding the Sun at its birth, by similar processes that eventually gave rise to life on Earth.

Not in every planetary system will life arise. What is needed is the right planet at the right distance around the right star. For instance, a planet that is too small will have insufficient gravity to retain the gases of its atmosphere, a fate which has befallen Mercury and, to a lesser extent, Mars. A planet needs to be about the size of the Earth or Venus before it can hold a suitable atmosphere. But having an atmosphere is not good enough if, like Venus, the planet is too close to the parent star. Venus has overheated; evaporation has removed all liquid water, which is essential for life as we know it. Mars, farther from the Sun than we are, is locked in the grip of ice. By good fortune, the Earth lies at the heart of the Sun's green belt, the area within which temperatures range neither too high nor too low for water to exist in liquid form. Of course, if the Sun were a larger, hotter star the green belt would correspondingly farther out, whereas if the Sun were smaller and cooler the green belt would be closer in.

So the planet's distance must be matched to the temperature of the star, but there is another consideration: the lifetime of the star. As we noted, the bigger and brighter a star is, the faster it burns out. We know from the evidence of our own existence that over four billion years is needed for life to evolve to an advanced state. Therefore big and bright stars are ruled out as centres of life, for they simply do not live long enough for evolution to progress. A star such as Sirius, with a mass twice that of the Sun, can live for only about a billion years, one-tenth the Sun's lifetime – hardly long enough for even the simplest cells to arise. A star with 25 per cent more mass than the Sun survives for about half the Sun's lifetime; if we had arisen around such a star, it would be burning out just about now.

On the other hand, stars smaller than the Sun live very much longer. But the drawback here is that such stars give out less heat and light than the Sun. A star with one-tenth the Sun's mass, such as the red dwarf Barnard's star, has a very narrow green belt which would not even reach the orbit of Mercury. The chances of finding a life-bearing planet around a dim red dwarf star seem negligible. Suitable stars to nurture life are those closely similar to the Sun, which possess the right combination of energy output and lifetime.

These restrictions considerably limit the number of sites for life, but that's just as well – if habitable planets circled every star the Galaxy would be suffering chronic over-population. Planets can be thought of as seeds scattered throughout the star fields of the Galaxy, only a few of which germinate. Once life on a planet takes root, it may then seed the rest of the Galaxy via space travel.

It remains a remarkable fact that the Universe is suited for life at all. For instance, if the force of gravity were only a few per cent stronger, stars such as the Sun would burn out too quickly for life to have evolved on

In some five billion years' time the Sun will gradually swell into a red giant one hundred times its present size. As this happens the Earth's atmosphere will disappear and the oceans boil away into space as our planet is consumed by the nuclear fires of the dying star.

Earth. If gravity were slightly weaker, the Sun would be a dim red dwarf unable to warm any planets – but planets would be unlikely too, for there might not be any supernovae to produce and scatter the required materials into space. Forces between atomic particles inside stars are similarly finely balanced; if these forces were slightly different from their current values the effects would be similar to those caused by changes in the strength of gravity. If the masses of atomic particles were different, chemistry and nuclear physics would be different, with consequent implications for the existence of life. Again, if there were slight alterations in the forces between atomic particles, all the hydrogen in the Universe would have been turned into helium in the hot Big Bang. In a Universe without hydrogen there would be no water, no long-lived stars like the Sun and, almost certainly, no life.

Furthermore, we are lucky that the Big Bang did not generate a lot more waste heat than it did. Space is cold, but it has a measurable temperature of -270°C. If the temperature of space were 100°C or above, liquid water could not exist anywhere and the chances of life would be virtually zero. Evidently the Universe has been expanding with a smooth uniformity since the Big Bang itself; any erratic motions or turbulence would have generated more heat than is observed. According to cosmologists, such an orderly expansion is highly unlikely – as unlikely as an entire crowd of people having spontaneously fallen into step. The Universe that we see seems to have curiously special properties.

We are also lucky that most of the matter in the Universe did not promptly disappear into the gravitational pit of black holes, which it would have done had the material of the Universe been denser than are the clouds which form stars and galaxies. On the other hand, if the matter in the Universe were more thinly spread than it is, stars and galaxies would not form, and again we would not be here to admire the result.

In short, the Universe seems tailor-made for life – or at least only a very limited range of adjustments could be made and still allow life to exist. Why did the Universe emerge from the Big Bang so admirably suited for life when all the odds seem to have been against it? One possibility is that the Universe really is unique, and was specially created for our benefit. If that is so, it seems a remarkably elaborate exercise, with a great deal of wasted space and a lot of pointless activity.

There are two other possibilities. One is that the Universe oscillates, periodically reprocessing itself through a new Big Bang to produce another Universe with a new set of laws. Therefore the Universe we perceive is just one of an endless series, virtually all the others of which are lifeless. Unfortunately for this theory, there is no sign that the current expansion of the Universe is going to slow down and give way to a subsequent contraction, as would be necessary to create another Big Bang.

The other possibility is even more astounding. According to some physicists, many alternative Universes exist, all rooted in the same Big Bang but differing in various ways. All these alternative Universes exist in parallel like so many books on an endless library shelf. We are characters in one of those books.

Some of the alternative Universes will be only slightly different from our own: perhaps Mars rather than the Earth would be the inhabitable planet of the solar system, or we might live around Alpha Centauri, not the Sun. But most of the alternative Universes would be of the hot, uninhabitable kind, populated not with radiant stars but black holes or a set of chemical elements that resolutely refused to bind together into living matter. We live in and know this particular Universe simply because its conditions are right for our existence. Perhaps we have other selves living in closely similar Universes.

Alas, there seems no way we can actually know of or contact these alternative Universes or our presumed other selves. It's not even clear whether, like the characters in a book, we have to accept the plot the way it is written, or whether we can change the outcome by our own free choice. Can we choose the Universe we live in, or has it in a sense chosen us? And since we live in a Universe seemingly so well suited for life, can we be its only inhabitants?

Chapter Five

SHUTTLING INTO SPACE

It was coincidental, but appropriate, that the Space Shuttle made its maiden flight into orbit on the 20th anniversary of Yuri Gagarin's pioneer venture – appropriate because the Shuttle heralds a new era in manned spaceflight as significant as that begun by Gagarin. The Shuttle opens the way to commuter trips into orbit, the building of space factories and the establishment of habitats capable of housing humans for extended periods. In short, the Shuttle is the start of the human colonization of space that will eventually spread life off Earth far beyond the Moon and planets, to the stars.

The Shuttle is launched like a rocket but lands like an aircraft. On April 12, 1981, astronauts John Young and Robert Crippen piloted the Space Shuttle Columbia into orbit from Cape Canaveral for its first test flight, gliding down to land two days later on a dry lakebed at Edwards Air Force Base in California. Seven months later, Columbia was in orbit again, thereby becoming the world's first reusable spacecraft. That reusability is the Shuttle's key to success.

Unlike previous rockets and spacecraft which were thrown away with each mission, the Shuttle orbiter is designed to be reused 100 times, thereby cutting the cost of spaceflight. As its name implies, the Shuttle's role is to ferry people and equipment between Earth and orbit. In addition to its astronaut pilots, the Shuttle can carry up to four selected passengers – scientists and engineers who will work in space. And it can bring expensive equipment back to Earth rather than having to abandon it up there as has been the rule to date.

The Shuttle orbiter, the part that actually carries the crew and cargo, is a winged vehicle 37.2 metres long, about the size of a DC 9 jet aircraft. At its nose is the flight deck and crew quarters in which the astronauts ride. Half the orbiter's length is taken up by the cargo bay which can handle payloads 18.3 metres long, 4.6 metres wide and weighing up to 29 tonnes – the equivalent in size and weight of two fully loaded double-decker buses.

At launch the orbiter is mated to a large external fuel tank, 47 metres long and 8.4 metres in diameter. This tank feeds liquid hydrogen and oxygen to the three main engines at the orbiter's rear. During the ascent, these engines are throttled to keep acceleration forces below 3 g, so as not to damage delicate payloads. For additional boost at launch, two solid-fuel rockets are strapped to the sides of the external tank. These burn out and fall away just over two minutes into the flight, parachuting back into the sea where they are recovered for reuse. Only the external fuel tank is not scheduled for reuse, despite the fact that, at 35 tonnes, it weighs more than the orbiter's payload. The fuel tank is jettisoned and burns up as the orbiter reaches the outer edge of the atmosphere.

Two smaller engines, known as the orbital manoeuvring system (OMS), give the orbiter

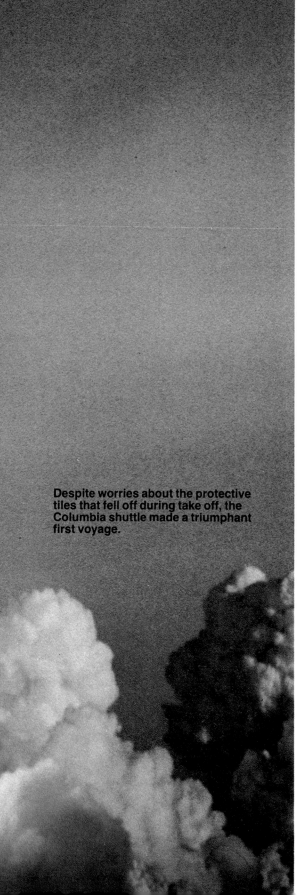

Despite worries about the protective tiles that fell off during take off, the Columbia shuttle made a triumphant first voyage.

its final push into orbit once the external tank is jettisoned. They are also used as retro-rockets to nudge the orbiter back to Earth when its mission is over.

Silica-fibre tiles glued to the orbiter's exterior protect it from the searing heat of re-entry. The re-entry trajectory is selected to keep deceleration forces to $1\frac{1}{2}$ g. Back in the atmosphere the orbiter's wings allow it to be flown to the landing site. Its engines do not operate during the descent, making it less like an aircraft than a glider weighing 85 tonnes (or more when carrying a payload).

The Shuttle orbits from 185 kilometres to 1000 kilometres above the Earth; its engines have no fuel to take it higher, and it is certainly not designed to go to the Moon. By the mid 1980s a fleet of four or five Shuttles will be making regular trips into orbit every few weeks. Many of these flights will carry a space station called Spacelab, built for NASA by the European Space Agency, which will be crewed by men and women from Europe as well as from the United States. Spacelab remains fixed in the Shuttle's cargo bay and is brought back to Earth after each week-long mission.

Spacelab consists of two main parts: a series of platforms open to the vacuum of space called pallets, on which instruments are mounted; and a cylindrical pressurized laboratory in which scientists work, carrying out experiments and operating the equipment on the pallets. Among Spacelab's wide range of applications, many will be of direct benefit to us here on Earth, such as surveys of our planet's land, oceans and atmosphere; biological studies in weightlessness; observations of the Sun to keep track of its minor variations and how they might affect Earth's climate; and manufacture of new materials such as alloys, glasses and pharmaceuticals that cannot be made under the pull of gravity.

For the first time it will be possible for scientists and engineers to travel into space along with their own scientific equipment. One of those people could be you. Imagine that you have applied to fly as an experimenter on Spacelab to carry out work that you have been planning with your colleagues in a university or industry research team.

Aboard Spacelab you will have to operate many other experiments in addition to your own, so you will require a wide scientific knowledge and versatile practical ability. You will not have to pilot the Shuttle – NASA's professional astronauts do that – but you must be fit, under the age of 50, and between 150 centimetres and 190 centimetres in height.

After having satisfied a selection board of your scientific and technical capabilities you are subjected to a series of psychological and medical tests to assess your suitability for spaceflight. The psychological tests establish your personality and emotional stability; the selection board is looking for people who can work as a team in a cramped spacecraft. Also tested are your memory, ability to reason clearly, motivation, and manual dexterity.

Doctors examine your eyesight, brain-wave patterns, heart and lungs. Your reaction to physical stress is checked as you walk a treadmill. You will sit in a spinning chair to test your susceptibility to motion sickness. You will be swung in a centrifuge to simulate the acceleration forces during launch. The lower body negative pressure cylinder will suck blood into the lower half of your body to simulate the effect on your body's circulation of your return to Earth's gravity from weightlessness.

Most excitingly, you will get a taste of weightlessness itself in a large cargo aircraft flying a roller-coaster trajectory. As it reaches the top of a curve and begins to fall you float weightless inside the aircraft's padded cabin for 30 seconds at a time. A test which some of your colleagues find particularly unpleasant involves the rescue sphere, an 86-centimetre diameter fabric ball in which you sit hunched up in the dark for half an hour. Rescue spheres will be used to transfer crew between Shuttles in space in the event of an emergency.

Having proved that you are mentally and physically capable of operating expensive equipment under the demanding conditions of spaceflight, you are accepted as a so-called Payload Specialist. Then begins the training for your flight, which may still be as much as two years away. During this time you and the other payload specialists assigned to the flight work closely with the scientists developing equipment for the mission. You familiarize yourself with the living quarters aboard the Shuttle in a full-scale mock-up, and you learn the basic safety rules for emergencies such as fire or depressurization. As the technical manuals and other paperwork builds up on your desk you begin to realize what an onerous task you have taken on. The pace of preparations quickens, and you see less and less of your family.

A full-time scientist-astronaut known as the mission specialist is the science officer and your superior on the flight. He or she joins you in training to supervise the planning of the work schedule so that all experiments on the flight can be successfully completed. For the last two months or so of your training you move to NASA's Johnson Space Center at Houston, where you rehearse the mission in simulators and get better acquainted with living in close proximity to your crewmates. This is probably the first opportunity you will get to meet the commander and co-pilot who will actually fly you into space and back again; you are reassured to learn that they have both made the trip many times before. Finally you move to Cape Canaveral where Spacelab is being loaded into the Shuttle's cargo bay.

Now it is launch day. A white bus with a blue stripe takes you and your crewmates out to launch pad 39, the historic site from which the Apollo missions to the Moon departed. Sixty metres above the palmetto palms, alligators, pelicans, and silver sands of Cape Canaveral, within sight of the Atlantic Ocean, you climb through the Shuttle's circular hatch and take your place on the flight deck. You are lying on your back, looking upwards through the six panoramic windows to the Florida sky.

In front of you sit the commander and the co-pilot. On your right is the mission specialist. As there is room for only four persons on the upper flight deck, your three payload specialist colleagues are strapped onto couches on the mid-deck /below. Over the commander's shoulder you can see three video screens displaying computer information in green. From among the mass of other dials

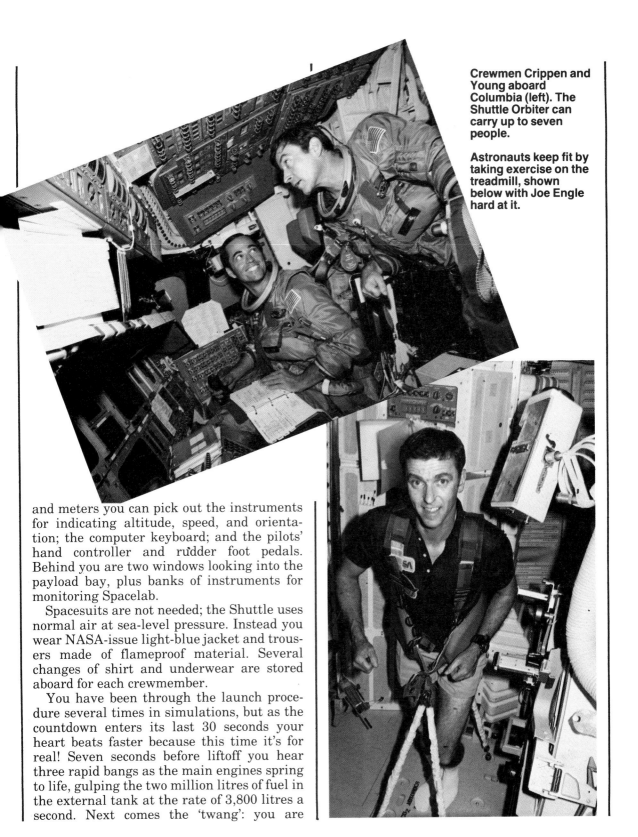

Crewmen Crippen and Young aboard Columbia (left). The Shuttle Orbiter can carry up to seven people.

Astronauts keep fit by taking exercise on the treadmill, shown below with Joe Engle hard at it.

and meters you can pick out the instruments for indicating altitude, speed, and orientation; the computer keyboard; and the pilots' hand controller and rudder foot pedals. Behind you are two windows looking into the payload bay, plus banks of instruments for monitoring Spacelab.

Spacesuits are not needed; the Shuttle uses normal air at sea-level pressure. Instead you wear NASA-issue light-blue jacket and trousers made of flameproof material. Several changes of shirt and underwear are stored aboard for each crewmember.

You have been through the launch procedure several times in simulations, but as the countdown enters its last 30 seconds your heart beats faster because this time it's for real! Seven seconds before liftoff you hear three rapid bangs as the main engines spring to life, gulping the two million litres of fuel in the external tank at the rate of 3,800 litres a second. Next comes the 'twang': you are

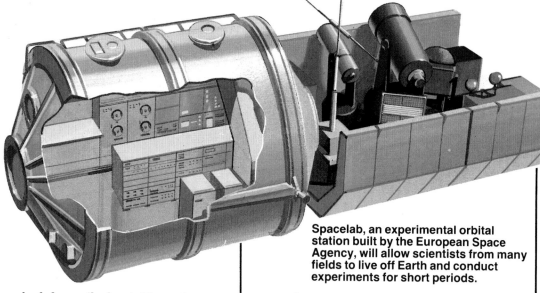

Spacelab, an experimental orbital station built by the European Space Agency, will allow scientists from many fields to live off Earth and conduct experiments for short periods.

gently rocked forward about 50 centimetres in your seat as the engines build up thrust and the whole vehicle bends slightly; then the Shuttle settles back again. With two loud explosions the solid rocket boosters ignite and the Shuttle starts to rise like a high-speed elevator. Out of the side windows you see the launch tower slipping past. You are off on your first trip into space.

In addition to the shaking and rattling produced by the solid boosters you notice a slightly disconcerting jiggling as the main engines swivel to steer the Shuttle on its programmed course. Only when the Shuttle punches through a low deck of cloud is there any sense of speed. Less than a minute after liftoff the Shuttle goes supersonic, and the ride becomes much smoother and quieter. As the Shuttle accelerates you feel your body weight build up to three times its normal Earth value – uncomfortable, but not painful. Through the windows, the sky turns from blue to black.

Two minutes into the flight you notice a slight deceleration as the solid rockets near the end of their fuel. For half a second the windows are filled by a bright yellow orange flame as the solid rockets are fired off from the sides of the external tank; out of the window you see them fall away. You are 50 kilometres high.

Now the ride becomes so smooth that if you closed your eyes you would hardly know you were moving. But in fact the shuttle is racing upwards at 5000 km/h, and the steadily increasing g-forces tell you it is still accelerating. Over the headset from Mission Control comes a brief call to confirm that the Shuttle is heading safely for orbit.

Six and a half minutes after the solid boosters were jettisoned the main engines cut off. Now you start to experience weightlessness. At first it feels as though you are hanging upside down. You float upwards in your seat, and you feel the blood rushing to your head, making your face puffy and your nose stuffy. While you are coming to terms with these strange sensations, the external tank is jettisoned to fall back into the atmosphere and burn up. Then the orbital manoeuvring system (OMS) engines fire to push the Shuttle gently into orbit. It has been 12 minutes since liftoff, and you have travelled little more than 200 kilometres upwards, yet it has been the most exciting journey of your life.

Now safely in orbit, you can relax and enjoy the view of Earth: snow-bright swirls of cloud overlying rich blue-green ocean, and the curve of the horizon against the intense blackness of space. Half an hour later the OMS engines are fired again to trim your orbit. It is time to begin work.

Gingerly you unstrap yourself and for the first time get the full feeling of weightlessness. Instinctively you reach out to grab hold of something to steady yourself, but you are floating without falling. Freed of the downward pull of gravity, your arms and shoulders hunch up, your knees bend and your arms float out in front of you. Looking at your fellow crewmen you see their puffy faces, hear their nasal voices, and notice their legs getting skinny, like crow's legs, as the fluids move into the upper parts of their bodies. Nasal congestion will remain with you throughout the flight, and may give you a headache during the first day in space. You might have taken a pill to prevent space sickness, but even so you are careful to avoid sudden head movements and resist the temptation to perform space acrobatics.

The co-pilot moves to the rear of the flight deck to open the Shuttle's cargo-bay doors. This is important both to expose Spacelab's instruments to space and also because the insides of the doors contain radiators which release waste heat from the Shuttle into space. When the air pressure in Spacelab has been checked you can open the hatch and pull yourself into the tunnel that links the Shuttle's mid-deck with Spacelab. You have rehearsed this many times on the ground, but now in unfamiliar weightlessness you find yourself pushing off too hard and running into the opposite wall. But soon you learn to control your movements.

The inside of Spacelab looks familiar from your many hours of training. There is a floor and ceiling to help you keep your bearings, while along either wall are racks of experimental equipment and control panels for the instruments mounted outside on the pallets. Overhead are windows and an airlock through which equipment can be pushed. To anchor yourself in position while working, your shoes have two suction cups on the soles.

Equipment on the pallets may include a telescope for analysing the ultraviolet light from stars or, if this is an Earth-pointing mission, the pallets may be equipped with cameras and radar for studying the Earth's atmosphere, land and oceans. Among your duties will be to aim the telescopes at required targets and take pictures. Other duties might include operating a furnace to make new metallic alloys or crystals of semiconductor materials for electronics. Other experiments exploiting the weightless environment of Spacelab may include the processing of super-pure drugs and vaccines, or watching the behaviour of cancerous cells in an attempt to discover reasons for their malignant nature. Some of the experiments will also involve medical tests on you and your companions, such as being rocked backwards and forwards on a device known as the Sled to discover more about the causes of motion sickness. This is likely to be one of the least popular duties.

The payload specialists will work alternate shifts in pairs; time in orbit is limited and expensive, so none is wasted. While at work in Spacelab, you can talk directly to scientists from the various research teams who are following your progress at the Payload Operations Control Centre in Houston. This support team will help sort out occasional troubles with instruments, discuss results to date, and suggest new observations based on some unexpected discovery.

When not at work in Spacelab you will live in the crew quarters in the mid-deck at the Shuttle's nose (the lowest deck of all is an underfloor space used for storage). As on a well-organized camping expedition, you will have to take your turn preparing the meals in the orbiter's galley, equipped with hot and cold water dispensers and an electric oven.

Three meals a day provide a daily intake of 3,000 calories per crewmember. Evening meal on your first day includes shrimp cocktail, steak with rice and broccoli, fruit cocktail and butterscotch pudding, washed down with a grape drink. You select the items on the menu from storage lockers, inject water into the shrimp, rice and broccoli, place the steak in the oven, and arrange the completed items on the food trays. Your companions join you for dinner around the mess table.

An hour is allowed for each meal. Afterwards you clean the cutlery and galley with wet cloths, and dump the garbage in bags through a hatch into the lower deck. A vacuum cleaner aids the housekeeping.

You have three quarters of an hour in the morning and in the evening for waking and washing or preparing for bed. Washing facilities consist of a small enclosed sink through which water is drawn by an airflow. You turn it on, adjust the water temperature, squirt some soap into your palm, and wash your hands. To wash other parts of your body you dampen a washcloth, then dry off with a towel. Each crewmember has his or her own kit containing toothbrush, soap, hairbrush and comb, nail clippers, and deodorant. Male crewmembers can choose a safety razor or a clockwork one.

The washing station and the orbital toilet are curtained off from the rest of the mid-deck. To use the toilet you close the privacy curtain, check the instructions on the wall, switch on the airflow, sit on the seat, hook your toes into foot restraints and swing two metal bars over your thighs to ensure you are firmly pressed down onto the seat. A rotating fan, called the slinger, flings solid wastes onto the commode wall where they are later dried by exposure to the vacuum of space. The urinal hose has a cup that makes it usable by males or females; it can be used in a standing or sitting position. Like an aircraft toilet, the Shuttle toilet is serviced when back on Earth.

You sleep zipped up in a sleeping bag in a bunk like a cupboard with a sliding door. But on this first night you are too excited to sleep at first, and you spend a few hours looking out of the windows on the flight deck, watching the world go by and taking tourist snaps, amazed at the detail of clouds, mountains, sand dunes, and rivers. Other off-duty relaxations include listening to taped music, challenging a computer at chess, or reviewing the following day's schedule. On the second night, though, you are so tired that you go to sleep almost immediately. Sleeping in weightlessness is comfortable and deeply relaxing, like being on a three-dimensional water bed.

Any spacewalks that are necessary during the flight, such as to service a jammed telescope or replace film packs, will be made by the mission specialist or the co-pilot, not by you. But you may have tried on one of the off-the-peg Shuttle spacesuits during training. It's a claustrophobic experience.

First comes the liquid-cooled undergarment which you zip yourself into like a boiler suit. It will keep you cool during even the most vigorous activities in space. There are no rest stops in space, so beneath the undergarment is a urine collection bag which is emptied after EVA. Over your head goes a soft cap containing headphones and a microphone for communication. Now you are ready to pull on the soft leggings of the spacesuit which come in a variety of sizes and are adjustable to suit virtually any crewmember. The hard upper torso of the suit is made of fibreglass, with soft sleeves, and comes in five sizes including extra-small for women. You wriggle up into it and connect it to the leggings by a metal waist ring. Bearings in the shoulder and arm joints give greater mobility than in the Apollo suits. The suited astronaut can bend, lean and twist more readily than ever before. Various insulating layers protect you against micrometeorites and heat, under a skin of Teflon-coated fibreglass.

On the back of the hard upper torso is the life-support system which provides oxygen and cooling water sufficient for a 6-hour spacewalk. A computerized chest-pack allows you to control and monitor the operation of the life-support system. Already you are starting to feel hot in the suit, so you switch on the cooling water and adjust its flow. Finally you pull on your gloves, chosen from a selection of 15 sizes, and clamp on your helmet. You are now totally enclosed and entirely reliant on the life-supporting backpack to prevent you from suffocating.

From inside your suit you can see the surrounding world through the plastic bubble helmet, but you don't feel very much a part of it. All you can hear comes crackling over the radio link. You breathe the odourless oxygen flowing through the suit. Your sense of touch is dulled by the thick gloves. And you must be prepared to spend several hours cooped up like this, without a chance of removing the helmet to snatch a breath of fresh air.

Astronauts exit into space through an airlock atop the tunnel leading into Spacelab. (When Spacelab is not flown, the airlock is affixed directly to the hatch from the mid-deck into the cargo bay.) To move around during an EVA, Shuttle astronauts use an armchair-like jet-propelled backpack. To don the backpack at its storage point on a bulkhead of the orbiter payload bay, the spacesuited astronaut simply backs into it; latches automatically snap it to the spacesuit. Hand

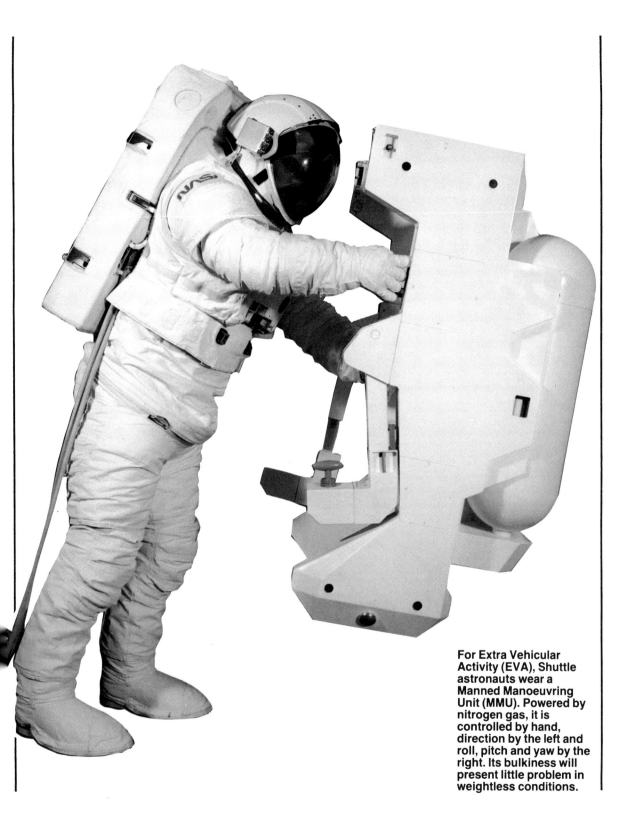

For Extra Vehicular Activity (EVA), Shuttle astronauts wear a Manned Manoeuvring Unit (MMU). Powered by nitrogen gas, it is controlled by hand, direction by the left and roll, pitch and yaw by the right. Its bulkiness will present little problem in weightless conditions.

controls in extendable arms either side of the backpack allow an astronaut to fire the backpack's thrusters. Each time a thruster fires, a warning tone sounds in the astronaut's headset. Thrust is provided by cold nitrogen gas which is replenished in the orbiter after each EVA. Equipped with such a jetpack, an astronaut can scoot around freely in space or help ferry colleagues from a crippled Shuttle to a rescue ship. In keeping with the Shuttle's philosophy of economy and reusability, each suit is cleaned and dried after use and should be good for a 15-year lifetime.

Life aboard Spacelab is exhausting, but scientifically rewarding. As you orbit the Earth, day and night sweep over the Shuttle every 1½ hours. After one hundred sunrises and the same number of sunsets, your week in space comes to an end – all too soon, it seems. You switch off the equipment aboard Spacelab, and the Shuttle commander closes the doors of the cargo bay securely around it. Reluctantly, you seal the hatchway leading into Spacelab and strap yourself into your seat in preparation for re-entry into the Earth's atmosphere.

Above Australia the commander turns the Shuttle so that it is travelling tail first; you feel a slight push as the orbital manoeuvring system engines slow the Shuttle for it to begin its drop back to Earth. In an hour's time you will be back on the ground. The commander pitches the Shuttle over until its nose is pointed 40 degrees up, ensuring that its insulated underside takes the heat of re-entry. Above the Pacific Ocean, 100 kilometres up and travelling at 25 times the speed of sound, you hit the upper edge of the atmosphere. Friction with the air creates a reddish-pink glow around the Shuttle, turning to orange near the nose where temperatures are hottest. It seems as though you are flying through a neon tube.

Despite the speed at which you are flying, the Shuttle's re-entry is very smooth, without a hint of turbulence. As the Shuttle slows, you feel as though you are being crushed by a great weight even though the maximum deceleration force is no more than 1½ g – after a week spent weightless you have forgotten what gravity feels like.

About half an hour after re-entry began the Shuttle is plunging in a steep glide towards the landing strip, descending at a rate of 3000 metres per minute, seven times steeper than the descent rate of a commercial jet. Residents of central Florida hear a double sonic boom as the Shuttle soars overhead, still well above normal air lanes. At an altitude of 6.4 kilometres it enters the restricted air space of the Kennedy Space Center at Cape Canaveral. It goes subsonic only four minutes before touchdown. Under control of a microwave landing system the Shuttle orbiter glides towards the runway, the pilots monitoring its performance on their video screens. Without engines, there is no opportunity to fly the Shuttle around and make a second approach. Fourteen seconds before touchdown, the wheels come down. There is scarcely a bump as the Shuttle glides onto the concrete runway at 346 km/h, fifty per cent faster than a commercial jet. It rolls for a further 3 kilometres before coming to a halt.

You feel relieved, and perhaps a little queasy, after the high-speed descent. But most noticeable of all is the sluggishness of your limbs under Earth's gravity, and the need to steady yourself for fear of unbalancing as you stand upright after the flight.

There is no hero's welcome, for orbital spaceflight is now routine. A bus takes you to the reception area where you are given a brief medical examination while the Shuttle orbiter is towed into a hangar. There the Spacelab in which you worked for the past week is lifted out and replaced by new instrumentation for the Shuttle's next flight on which some other privileged scientist will take the role of payload specialist that you have just experienced. For you, now begins the much longer task of analysing the valuable data that you and your instruments have collected.

That is a typical space mission of the late 1980s and early 1990s. At present, Shuttle flights are limited to a maximum of seven days by the electrical power available in the orbiter, supplied by three fuel cells. Additional power could be provided by solar panels which unfurl in orbit, supporting Spacelab missions up to a month long.

Beyond that, NASA has plans for a large space station, known as the Space Operations Centre (SOC). This would be built up from sections similar to Spacelab, ferried into orbit by the Space Shuttle and plugged together to provide accommodation and working space for the crew. Such an orbital waystation, 350 kilometres above the Earth, could act as a maintenance depot for satellites, a checkout and refuelling stop for Shuttles and other payloads destined for higher orbits, and be a construction centre for structures too large to be carried into orbit in one piece by the Shuttle. Chief among these will be antennae several hundred metres across for communications, plus solar panels to 'farm' the Sun's energy for transmission back to Earth.

Automatic beam builders will be used to form latticework girders from cartridges of aluminium strips. Such beams would be unable to support themselves under Earth's gravity, but in weightless space all sorts of hefty equipment can be anchored to these thin trellises. Construction workers will fly around in pods with remotely-controlled

Scientists on Earth have built robot beam builders, but will these devices work in space, where the effects of weightlessness may prove less beneficial than has been hoped?

arms, like in the film *2001*.

Prototype beam-building robots have already been tried out on Earth. In space, such a machine could string together a kilometre-long beam in less than a day. But construction of large space structures raises a number of engineering questions. Will expansion of a beam in sunlight and subsequent contraction when in shadow set up stresses that could warp or even shatter it? The solution might be to use ultra-low-expansion plastics. Long beams would vibrate like tuning forks when knocked. In the weightless vacuum of space, such vibrations would not die out. What can be done to prevent a vibrating beam from shaking itself to pieces?

These basic structural problems, similar to those that afflicted pioneering bridge builders, must be solved successfully before orbiting space bases become a reality.

Chapter Six

NEW FRONTIERS IN SPACE

Cities in the sky, bases on the Moon and planets, and travel to the stars. This is the stuff of science fiction that is about to become fact. Less than a human lifetime from now, space colonies capable of containing as many people as a football stadium will be orbiting high above the Earth. Tens of thousands of people could be spending their entire lives off the Earth next century, giving birth to new generations for whom home will be out there, not down here.

Space colonies and Moon bases are inextricably linked, for it is on the Moon that we will find the materials with which to build in space. When geologists on Earth analysed the rocks brought back by the Apollo astronauts, they found that the Moon contains useful amounts of aluminium, iron, titanium, and magnesium. There is also plenty of silica for glassmaking. Large-scale space industries will be supported by raw materials from the Moon, and later from asteroids. These riches will make space industries independent of the Earth, and ensure abundant supplies even when the Earth's resources are depleted. Next century, top-quality goods from space factories will be flowing into the shops of Earth. It is not surprising that Japan and Germany are both very interested in the possibilities of manufacturing in space.

The first lunar base would probably consist of a few pressurized cylinders burrowed a little way under the lunar surface for insulation, similar to one of the scientific bases in Antarctica. A likely spot is in the southeastern Mare Tranquillitatis, near the crater Maskelyne, where lowland soils rich in iron and titanium as well as highland rocks containing aluminium are available. At Moon Quarry One, a small group of Moon miners would scoop up the lunar surface, pack it into fibreglass bags and fire it off into space along a magnetic launcher known as a mass driver.

One of the advantages of the Moon is its low gravity, which means that powerful rockets are not necessary to take off from it – witness the relatively feeble lunar module of Apollo days. In fact, a rocket is not necessary at all. A powerful catapult could do the job, since there is no atmosphere to resist very high speeds at ground level. A mass driver is really a magnetic catapult. Bags of lunar ore would be dumped into metal buckets which are then accelerated by magnetic forces along the mass-driver track, 2 kilometres long. When moving at lunar escape velocity, 2.4 km/sec,

An artist's impression of a communications and staging base on Deimos, the diminutive Martian moon only 12 kilometres in diameter. Gravity would be so low that there would be a danger of energetic movements sending an unwary astronaut into orbit.

the payload is ejected and the buckets return to the filling station to be reloaded.

A Moon base, operated by 50 personnel, could mine over half a million tons of lunar ores each year and fire it into space where it would be caught in a large net and hauled by space freighter to a processing plant. There the valuable metals would be extracted from the ores by techniques modified from those used in industry on Earth. Incidentally, such mining will not despoil the Moon. A lunar quarry could operate for 50 years without producing a crater large enough to be seen by telescopes on Earth. Since the Moon is such a rich source of raw materials it seems inevitable that certain industries will be set up there rather than in space.

A network of small pressurized cylinders – essentially underground space stations – may be suitable for a small colony of Moon miners, who will accept spartan conditions similar to those on offshore oil rigs in return for financial rewards. But something altogether more elaborate is required for larger communities. For one thing, it will be psychologically restricting not to have a view of the outside, so

A typical lunar colony would support up to 200 people. Mining would be its major industry but there would also be a farm and a scientific station. Visiting the lunar colony by Shuttle would be a simple business.

transparent domes may become a feature of lunar architecture.

In conjunction with NASA, two young architects at the University of Houston, John Dossey and Guillermo Trotti, have designed a lunar base called Counterpoint, which they site in St George crater near the Apollo 15 landing location, at the foot of the lunar Apennine mountains. Base Counterpoint will grow in ten years from an outpost for 15 to 20 people to a full-scale, self-sufficient colony of 200 persons.

Counterpoint has a central spine to which additional sections are plugged in. Each part of Counterpoint can be isolated by airlocks in the event of a pressure loss. Oxygen to breathe is extracted in a processing plant from lunar soil, which contains liberal amounts of oxygen locked up chemically. Because of the two-week-long lunar night, solar power is not really practical on the Moon, so power for the base will be provided by an underground nuclear reactor. Sufficient light for surface activities during the night should be provided by the Earth, for Earthlight is 50 times stronger than Moonlight.

Counterpoint will have a farm, a research area, an industrial plant, a civic centre, and a chapel. Much of Counterpoint will be built from lunar materials, such as basalt rock melted and cast in the industrial complex, as well as metals extracted from the rocks. To reach Counterpoint you will first take a Shuttle to an Earth-orbital station. There, another Shuttle will ferry you to orbit around the Moon, from where Counterpoint's own tugs will pick you up for the trip down to one of the base's landing pads. After landing, the tug will move along a track to a refuelling station, or if maintenance is required it will be lowered on an elevator into a subsurface pressurized hangar.

Meanwhile, you enter the pressurized main corridor of the colony. Extending off to your right is the industrial area, largely unpressurized and automatic, in which lunar rocks are processed to provide raw materials for the colony. Ahead of you is the civic centre, a pressurized dome nine storeys high and spanning 68.5 metres. This is Counterpoint's recreational centre, where sporting events will take place in the low lunar gravity. On the various levels of the civic centre are a cinema, theatre and art gallery, swimming pools, restaurants and landscaped gardens. Each day the pre-programmed weather can be changed. Views of clouds, the Earth, or anywhere in space can be projected onto the inside of the dome to provide a richness of visual environment that the Moon lacks.

Through the dome of the civic centre rises a basalt tower topped with communications antennae and housing the administrative centre of the colony. Here, computers monitor the operation of the entire complex and air traffic controllers watch the arrival and departure of tugs to and from orbit. On the ground, you see lunar vehicles running over the dusty surface carrying exploration and work teams. From the control tower, a pressurized bridge leads you past administrative offices to another basalt tower containing

conference rooms and the library, topped by the chapel with a transparent dome to contemplate the wonders of the heavens.

The towers at Counterpoint provide good views, but they are exposed to radiation from the Sun and cosmic rays from the Galaxy. Living quarters are totally shielded from such radiation, being tunnelled out of the lunar rock five metres below the surface. The warren-like residences are divided into apartments for one to four people, allowing individuals, groups, or families to live together, including accommodation for a number of visitors. Many of the visitors will be scientists who have come to conduct experiments in the laboratory complex. Looking rather like a merry-go-round, the laboratory consists of various plug-in units attached to a tower. Each module is a space station, fitted out on Earth and then ferried to the Moon where it is plugged into the core which provides the necessary life-support systems.

Let's visit the lunar farm. Lunar soil, with added water, fertilizer, and perhaps a few earthworms, makes a remarkably good growing medium, as scientists found when they raised plants successfully in soil returned by the Apollo astronauts. On the Moon the best crop would be soybeans because of their high protein content and ease of growth. Food technologists have already produced artificial meat made from soybeans, so perhaps soybean steaks will be among the delicacies at Counterpoint's dinner tables.

The lunar farm will be enclosed under a dome containing a low-pressure atmosphere of carbon dioxide and nitrogen, with artificial illumination. The soybeans grow in large trays and can be harvested automatically by machine. A smaller dome containing normal atmosphere contains runs for 200 chickens, 50 goats, and ponds for thousands of catfish and trout.

Beyond the Moon, the most likely target for manned visits is the planet Mars. The first manned voyages to Mars might take place around the year 2001, when Earth and Mars make one of their periodic close approaches. Two ships would depart on the long haul to Mars, built from components ferried into orbit

by Shuttles. Each craft carries a crew of six but can take on board the crew of the other vessel should it become disabled. Living quarters are in a cylinder about 15 metres long, slightly larger than the Skylab space station. Behind this are nuclear or electric rockets that propel the ship towards Mars.

The outward journey takes perhaps six months. Surveying the planet from orbit, the crew send down automatic probes to test potential landing sites. At the tip of each manned ship is a conical Mars landing craft looking like an enlarged Apollo capsule, 9 metres wide and weighing 40 tonnes. In these, three members of each crew make a rocket-powered descent to the surface.

For the next month the astronauts will roam the red sands of Mars, making daily excursions in an electric car to collect rocks and make geological maps. When their explorations are over, the astronauts return in the top half of the Mars lander to rejoin the mother ship orbiting above. Then they set course for home, arriving back 16 months after they set out.

Bases on Mars would follow a similar pattern to lunar bases. With an iron content of 12 to 16 per cent in its surface rocks, Mars must be the richest source of iron ore in the solar system apart from metal meteorites. But no one is designing Mars bases yet.

Of all the habitats that have been suggested for human life off Earth, the most revolutionary are the space colonies of Gerard O'Neill, a professor of physics at Princeton, New Jersey. At the time when project Apollo was grinding to a halt, in the early 1970s, O'Neill developed the concept of artificial worlds in space, enclosed spheres or cylinders on whose inner surfaces many thousands of humans could live. Pressurized with Earth-type air and illuminated by sunlight, each colony would spin to provide an artificial sense of

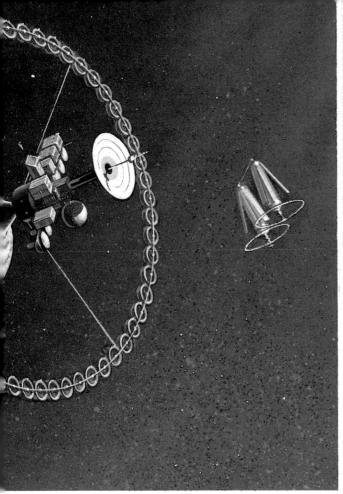

gravity on its inner surface, like a fairground centrifuge.

O'Neill was quick to realize that such colonies would best be built from materials mined from the Moon and shot into space by a mass driver. In conjunction with engineers at the Massachusetts Institute of Technology, O'Neill built and demonstrated the first working model of a mass driver in 1977. It is largely due to his insights that the concepts of lunar mining and space habitation are so advanced. During the decade of the seventies, O'Neill mapped out humanity's future in space.

The prospects are awesome. In his book about the world next century, 2081, O'Neill says: 'Once we break out from the confines of the planet, we can begin building new lands from the limitless resources of our solar system, and can use freely as much as we need of the sunlight that now streams out, wasted, into the cold darkness beyond the planets.'

Island 3 (left), one of O'Neill's visions of life off Earth, could have a self-sufficient population of several millions. The cylinders rotate to create artificial gravity and sunlight entering the colony is controlled by adjustable mirrors creating an Earth-like interior (above).

For the first colony, known as Island One, O'Neill envisages an aluminium sphere 500 metres in diameter, with walls as thick as an armour-plated battleship – up to 20 centimetres. Its structural mass will be 100,000 tonnes, equivalent to that of a large ocean liner, although the buildings and soil within it will weigh several times more. It will need to be shielded from cosmic rays by an outer shell containing three million tonnes of slag left over from processing lunar soil.

Island One will be big enough to stand the Empire State Building in. And even though it is the smallest of the colony designs, it could contain 10,000 people without overcrowding. Detailed engineering calculations have shown that not only is construction of such a colony physically possible, but that spheres up to 20 kilometres in diameter are feasible within the known strength of materials. These could house millions of people.

Island One will rotate twice a minute to provide Earth-like gravity. Rotation at this speed would be noticeable to the inhabitants as they moved around on the inner surface of the sphere, and some people might find the feeling slightly discomforting, producing motion sickness. But the larger a colony, the slower it need rotate to provide Earth gravity, so in the largest colonies the spinning sensation will be too slight to cause problems.

The effect of artificial gravity in a rotating colony diminishes as you approach its axis of rotation. In practice, therefore, only the part of the sphere around the equator will experience full Earth gravity. Halfway from the equator to the axis of rotation, the effect of gravity will have dropped by one-third, and this will probably be the limit of the inhabited area. As you walk the rest of the way to the axis, you will feel progressively lighter, ending up weightless at the axis itself. Here will be opportunities for novel forms of recreation that utilize the unusual conditions of a space colony. Space colonies could become fascinating places for an adventure holiday, like Disneyworld in space. A lettergram from such a colony next century might be like the example on page 79.

Larger colonies than Island One will probably be cylindrical in shape, so that most of the land area will be at full Earth gravity. The largest such design, which O'Neill terms Island Three, could be 7 kilometres in diameter, 32 kilometres long, and capable of housing millions of people.

What is the point of such colonies? They will grow out of orbital bases such as the Space Operations Center, and will provide refuelling stops for long-distance spacecraft as well as living accommodation for workers in space factories. It seems likely that many industries will move off Earth in the coming centuries, particularly those that require large amounts of energy. Once the first colony is constructed, each new one can be built by the inhabitants of the first. Communities of

One of the most popular designs for space colonies is the wheel-like torus which spins to create artificial gravity. The original Stanford torus was designed in 1975. An amended version produced by D. J. Sheppard uses fused lunar rock, or 'mooncrete', instead of metal as the main building material.

scientists are going to relish the idea of a purpose-built science colony in orbit. And a space colony will, of course, be an ideal place to build spaceships, either for simple ferry missions to the Moon or for voyages to the stars.

Most importantly, space colonies are independent of the Earth, so whatever happens on this planet – starvation, disease, nuclear war – will not affect the prospects of the space dwellers. We are on the verge of a fundamental split of humanity into two distinct races: planet people, who remain on Earth, and space people, who leave to take up residence on the offshore islands of space colonies.

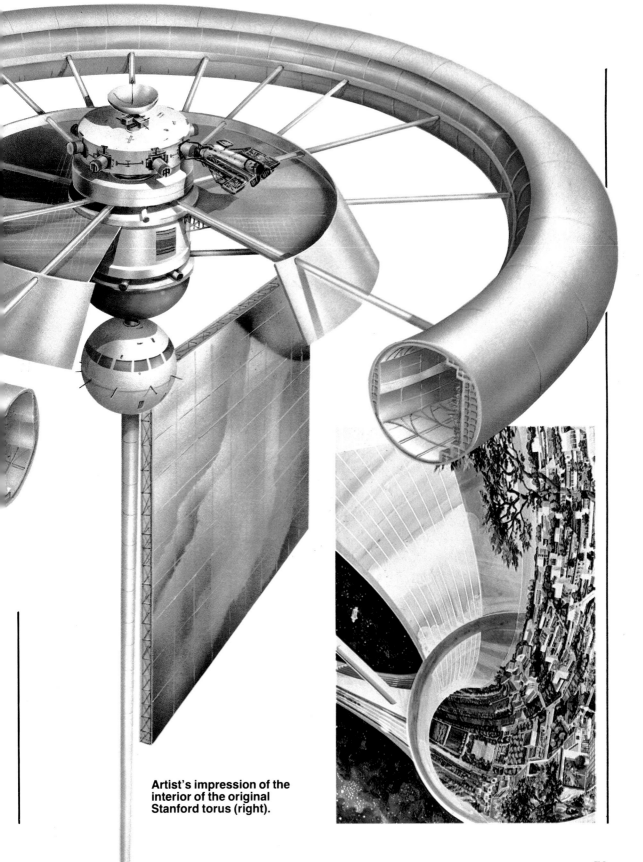

Artist's impression of the interior of the original Stanford torus (right).

The increasing independence of colonies from Earth will be reflected in their location. At first, colonies such as Island One will orbit between Earth and Moon, where they are accessible from both bodies. Construction of space colonies may produce one of the most remarkable real-estate booms in history, with the Shuttles of next century packed with emigrants eager to take up residence in the new worlds of space. Other colonies will start to spring up at the richest source of raw materials in the solar system, the asteroid belt. There, almost pure chunks of iron and nickel are to be found, as well as substances such as carbon and hydrogen in which the Moon is lacking and from which plastics can be made. Given large enough mirrors to collect sunlight, space colonies could exist anywhere within the solar system, as far away as the orbit of Pluto. The potential for the spread of life off Earth is as unlimited as the material riches of space itself.

The main disadvantage of other planets as homes for humans is that none of them has the right conditions for us. Throughout history, mankind has attempted to change his environment to suit himself, and this principle might even be extended to modifying entire planets. If a planet is not sufficiently Earthlike then we might make it so by a process termed terraforming.

To some people, terraforming suggests technological megalomania. Most alarming of all the schemes is the one which involves setting off nuclear explosions on the Moon to liberate oxygen from its rocks and so build up an atmosphere around our satellite. Another way of accomplishing the same result would be to bake the oxygen out of the lunar rocks by focusing the Sun's heat on them with mirrors. Water could be imported in the form of an icy comet or by icebergs scooped from the frozen rings of Saturn. The idea of our Moon with seas, an atmosphere, and even its own clouds and weather sounds fantastic — yet it is possible. A sufficiently dense atmosphere would leak away only slowly, over thousands of years, so there would be no difficulty in keeping it topped up. Unfortunately, an atmosphere around the Moon would make it impossible to operate a mass driver on the surface because of air resistance, thereby nullifying one of the Moon's main advantages to us. For that reason alone, the Moon is likely to be left as it is.

Venus has always attracted the terraformers, because it is virtually the same size as the Earth and it has a dense atmosphere to work with. Professor Carl Sagan of Cornell University has described how bacteria, specially bred to resist the sulphuric acid of its clouds, could be seeded into the atmosphere of Venus to break down the planet's carbon dioxide atmosphere, releasing free oxygen. As the atmosphere cleared, temperatures would drop. Water and other gases would have to be imported from the outer solar system. By crashing comets and asteroids onto Venus, the planet's rate of spin could be speeded up until its day was similar to Earth's.

Mars has the problem of insufficient atmosphere which terraformers must overcome. One way might be to trigger the volcanoes of Mars by nuclear bombs so that they erupt more gases. More realistic would be to focus sunlight onto the polar caps of Mars, melting them to release water and carbon dioxide gas. Experiments by the Viking space probe showed that copious amounts of oxygen, locked up in the planet's soil, are released when the surface is wetted. So as water flows on Mars, a new atmosphere may gush from its soil. It should not be difficult to breed modified forms of plants and bacteria that could thrive on Mars, thereby hastening its transformation into an Earth-like planet.

At present these fantastic visions of terraforming are in the realm of science fiction, and they may always remain so. For one thing, the development of space colonies will make planetary surfaces irrelevant as habitats. And there is surely something abhorrent about destroying the environment of an entire planet because it does not meet human requirements. Modify a planet, and you wipe

The familiar scene of a city at night, set against the jagged scenery of the moon Tethys and the looming bulk of its parent planet Saturn, gives a vivid impression of terraforming. In fact, Venus and Mars would be the most likely candidates for such a venture.

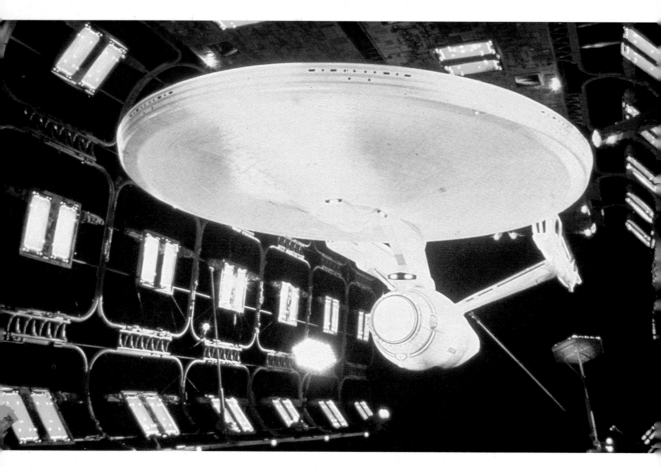

out over four billion years of geological history. It is doubtful that we shall undertake terraforming of the planets of the solar system, although someone else, somewhere out there might do it to other planets.

So far no mention has been made of the stars, but it is perhaps time to start thinking about them because next century we will be on our way there, too. Or at least robot probes will be. Already, four probes from Earth are on their way to the stars, though admittedly that is not the purpose for which they were built. They are Pioneers 10 and 11 and Voyagers 1 and 2, all of which were sent to study the outer planets of our solar system. As an inevitable consequence of their high-speed outward flight they will continue to move away from the Sun, drifting out into the Galaxy until contact is eventually lost with them.

So great are the distances between stars that if any of these probes were aimed at the nearest star, Alpha Centauri (and they are not), it would take them the best part of 100,000 years to get there. In practice, these probes will be lost in the unimaginable gulfs between stars, unless some alien explorers chance upon them. Existing rockets are not powerful enough to make much impression on that depressingly long transit time to the stars. We need new types of rocket for interstellar travel.

Fortunately, nuclear energy makes travel to the stars a practical possibility. For a given weight of fuel, nuclear reactions like those in a hydrogen bomb release 50 million times as much energy as do chemical reactions in conventional rockets. With such energy sources in mind, a team of engineers and physicists from the British Interplanetary Society has designed a prototype starship

Voyaging into fantasy –
Captain Kirk's starship
Enterprise (left). A real
starship would need
40,000 times its own
weight in fuel to
approach the speed of
light. The prototype
Daedalus, designed by
the British Interplanatary
Society, is designed to
travel at one tenth the
speed of light and
requires only 20 times its
own weight in fuel.
Assembled in space and
using 'fuel' extracted
from Jupiter, Daedalus
could reach the nearest
stars within a human
lifetime.

called Daedalus that could reach the nearest stars within a human lifetime, using technology likely to be available next century.

Unless there is some way around the laws of physics, interstellar journeys will always take many years, simply because stars are light years apart. To accelerate a starship to a speed close to that of light would require prohibitively large amounts of fuel, even using nuclear energy, and that is without considering the prospect of stopping it again. Travel close to the speed of light raises the problem of collisions with dust and gas particles in space, which at such speeds would have the destructive effect of a small bomb. It seems, therefore, that we must be content with planning interstellar voyages at about one-tenth the speed of light. This should be satisfactory enough, since it is 2000 times faster than today's probes.

Starships are going to be big by the standards of today's rockets; there is no doubt that they will have to be built in space out of raw materials extracted from the Moon and planets. Daedalus is an unmanned two-stage craft 230 metres long (twice the length of a Saturn V) and weighing over 50,000 tonnes (the equivalent of 18 Saturn Vs). Its most impressive feature is the huge hemispherical combustion chamber of its first stage, 100 metres in diameter, in which occur the nuclear fusion reactions which propel the craft.

The 'fuel' of Daedalus consists of pellets of deuterium (a heavy isotope of hydrogen) and helium-3 (a light isotope of helium). To get sufficient deuterium and helium-3 to fuel Daedalus we will need to sift the gaseous atmosphere of Jupiter, for there is nothing like enough of it nearer home. The fuel pellets, each about the size of a table-tennis ball, are stored ready-made in the craft's spherical fuel tanks, from where they are pumped at the rate of 250 every second into the combustion chamber. There, each pellet is blasted by a beam of electrons which compresses and heats the pellet, setting off a fusion reaction. The pellet explodes like a hydrogen bomb with a force of 90 tonnes of TNT. A strong magnetic field in the combustion chamber absorbs the force of the blast and pushes the craft along like a magnetic spring.

This may sound a hair-raising procedure, but it appears to be the most feasible way of releasing the required nuclear energy with foreseeable technology. The knowledge to design and build such a starship fusion drive probably exists in the nuclear research laboratories of the world, where it is classified for security reasons because of its application to nuclear weapons. Further developments in fusion research could provide an improved starship engine.

Daedalus will light up its fusion engine somewhere in the far reaches of the solar system, safely away from the Earth. After two years of boost the first stage is jettisoned and the propulsion is taken over for the next 1.8 years by the smaller second stage. This works in the same way as the first stage, but has a combustion chamber 40 metres in diameter. Daedalus will reach the impressive top speed of 130 million km/h, 12 per cent the speed of light, at which it coasts towards its target. At the front of Daedalus, protected by a metal shield to ward off impacts by cosmic particles, is the payload module containing 450 tonnes of sub-probes which will fan out on command of the master computer to investigate interstellar space, the target star, and any planets it may have.

A likely target for Daedalus is Barnard's star. This is the second closest star to the Sun, lying 6 light years away, and it might well have planets similar to Jupiter and Saturn. The total journey time to Barnard's star, from ignition to arrival, is just over 49 years. Since there is no fuel to slow Daedalus down, the sub-probes must snatch what information they can as they speed through the Barnard's star system in less than a day.

Each sub-probe radios its results to the Daedalus mother ship which then relays the information to radio telescopes on Earth. Of course, because Barnard's star is 6 light years distant the radio messages from Daedalus take 6 years to reach Earth. Results from the stars will not come quickly, even with fusion-powered probes; but it seems certain that future generations will marvel at colour pictures of planets around other stars as we have marvelled at the Voyager pictures of Jupiter and Saturn. Our descendants will see star-spots on Alpha Centauri and perhaps gaze on

25.08.2083/87.3542/SW24.03.297

SPACEGRAM NO: S/0089/SW2376.59875/6

ADDRESSEE: MR AND MRS GIBBONS
              89 WOODSTOCK STREET
              LONDON NW16 4QT
              UK 4596
              EARTH 213

FROM: JILLY AND JOHN GIBBONS
              MODULE 978/QT
              DELTA AVENUE 75
              SKYWORLD ONE 3102

GRAM ADDRESS SKYONE

DEAR MUM AND DAD

JOHN AND I GOT TO CANAVERAL SPACEPORT IN PLENTY OF TIME FOR
OUR SHUTTLE FLIGHT. THE MODERN PASSENGER SHUTTLES ARE DIRECT
DESCENDANTS OF THE CARGO SHUTTLES THAT FIRST FLEW FROM HERE
WHEN GRANDFATHER WAS A BOY. THE PART OF THE SHUTTLE IN
WHICH THE CARGO USED TO GO IS NOW A PRESSURIZED COMPARTMENT
LIKE AN AIRLINER FOR 100 PEOPLE, AND OUR FLIGHT WAS FULL.

DURING OUR PRE-FLIGHT BRIEFING WE HAD BEEN WARNED TO EXPECT
THREE LOUD BANGS AS THE ROCKET ENGINES IGNITED - THEN WE
WERE OFF% THE MOST DISCONCERTING EFFECT CAME SHORTLY AFTER
TAKE-OFF AS THE SHUTTLE ROLLED THROUGH 120° TO SET US ON
COURSE OUT OVER THE ATLANTIC - THROUGH THE WINDOWS IT LOOKED
AS THOUGH THE OUTSIDE WORLD WAS SPINNING AROUND. IT WASNT
LONG BEFORE WE SAW THE SKY TURN BLACK.   WE COULD FEEL THE
                                       MAIN ENGI
NES THROTTLE BACK TO PREVENT THE ACCELERATION
FORCES FROM BECOMING TOO GREAT. EVEN SO, IT FELT AS THOUGH
A HEAVY HAND WAS PRESSING ME DOWN IN MY SEAT. MY ARMS AND
LEGS FELT OVER TWICE AS HEAVY AS NORMAL WHEN I TRIED TO
MOVE THEM.

LESS THAN TEN MINUTES AFTER TAKE-OFF THE SHUTTLES ENGINES
SWITCHED OFF AND THE BIG FUEL TANK WAS DISCARDED. WE WERE
IN ORBIT AROUND THE EARTH, AND WE BEGAN TO FLOAT UPWARDS IN
OUR SEATS AS WE BECAME WEIGHTLESS. IT WAS AN AMAZING
FEELING, LIKE BEING BUOYED UP IN AN INVISIBLE TANK OF WATER,
BUT WE WERENT ALLOWED TO UNSTRAP OURSELVES AND ENJOY IT TO
THE FULL. WHEN JOHN AND I LOOKED AT EACH OTHER WE LAUGHED,
BECAUSE IN WEIGHTLESSNESS YOUR FACE CHANGES SHAPE - IN
PARTICULAR, YOUR CHEEKS PUFF OUT. ITS A BIT LIKE LOOKING
IN ONE OF THOSE DISTORTING MIRRORS AT A FAIRGROUND. WE HAD
BEEN WARNED NOT TO MOVE OUR HEADS AROUND TOO MUCH, BECAUSE
SOME PEOPLE GET SICK EARLY IN THEIR FLIGHT IF THEY DO THAT.
      %%%
I CANT DESCRIBE HOW BEAUTIFUL THE EARTH LOOKS FROM 200 KM
UP. THE SEAS ARE MANY SHADES OF BLUE AND GREEN, THE CLOUDS
ARE BRILLIANT WHITE, AND SNOW-TOPPED MOUNTAINS LOOK LIKE
LACE EMBROIDERY. JOHN, WHO HAD HOGGED THE WINDOW SEAT,
SAID HE SPOTTED ROADS AND THE WAKES OF SHIPS AT SEA. EVEN
I COULD CLEARLY SEE THE CURVATURE OF THE EARTH. SOON WE
SAW THE MOST GLORIOUS SUNSET - A BRILLIANT RAINBOW BAND OF
COLOURS ON THE HORIZON.

AS THE SHUTTLE MOVED OVER THE NIGHT SIDE OF EARTH I COULD
SEE CITY LIGHTS BELOW - I THINK I SPOTTED THAT NEW EXPERIMENTAL
OFFSHORE CITY NEAR INDIA. OCCASIONAL FLASHES OF LIGHTNING
LIT UP THE CLOUDS BELOW. AFTER FORTY FIVE MINUTES OF
DARKNESS THE SUN ROSE AGAIN, DAZZLING JOHN WHO WAS LOOKING
STRAIGHT AT IT.

DURING OUR ORBIT OF THE EARTH THE CAPTAIN HAD BEEN CHECKING
OUT THE SHUTTLE BEFORE STARTING UP ITS SMALLER ENGINES TO
PUSH US UP HIGHER TOWARDS THE SPACE COLONY THEY CALL SKYWORLD
ONE. IT LOOKS EVEN STRANGER IN REALITY THAN IT DOES IN
PHOTOGRAPHS. AS YOU KNOW, ITS A GIANT SPHERE SURROUNDED
BY A RING OF MIRRORS TO REFLECT IN SUNLIGHT THROUGH WINDOWS.
I WAS SURPRISED BY HOW GREEN THE AGRICULTURAL AREAS LOOKED -
THESE ARE GLASSHOUSES AROUND THE ENTRANCE TO THE SPHERE,
WHERE SKYWORLDS FOOD IS GROWN. SPACE, WE WERE TOLD ON THE
INFLIGHT VIDEO, IS AN IDEAL PLACE FOR GARDENING= THERES
NO SHORTAGE OF SUNLIGHT. PRESSURIZED GREENHOUSES, PLUS
WATER AND NITROGEN, ARE ALL YOU NEED.

A LOT OF SMALLER CRAFT WERE BUZZING AROUND SKYWORLD, TAKING
WORKERS TO AND FROM THE SPACE FACTORIES WHERE MICROELECTRONICS
AND MEDICINES ARE MADE. A BIG SPACE FREIGHTER WAS DUE FROM
%%   THE MOON, BRINGING SUPPLIES OF RAW MATERIALS TO START
BUILDING MORE COLONIES LIKE SKYWORLD. THE CAPTAIN DOCKED
THE SHUTTLE CAREFULLY AT ONE OF THE +POLES+ OF SKYWORLD,
AND AT LAST WE WERE ABLE TO FLOAT OUT, STILL WEIGHTLESS,
THROUGH AN AIRLOCK INTO THE CUSTOMS AND IMMIGRATION AREA.

IT SEEMS INCREDIBLE, BUT WORLDS IN THE SKY LIKE THIS WERE
FIRST PREDICTED OVER 100 YEARS AGO, WAY BACK IN THE 1970S,
BY AN AMERICAN PHYSICS PROFESSOR, GERARD ONEILL. HE
PROPOSED BUILDING A COLONY JUST LIKE THIS ONE, ABOUT 500
METRES ACROSS AND SPINNING TWICE A MINUTE TO PROVIDE
ARTIFICIAL GRAVITY ON ITS INNER SURFACE. DESPITE ALL THAT
WE KNEW ABOUT SKYWORLD IN ADVANCE, IT WAS STILL STRANGE TO
BEGIN MOVING ABOUT ON THE INSIDE SURFACE OF THE SPHERE,
LIKE THE EARTH TURNED INSIDE OUT.

WE WERE TAKEN ALONG THE SHORT TRIP TO OUR HOTEL BY ELECTRIC
BUS - SKYWORLD IS KEPT POLLUTION FREE AND, AS FAR AS
POSSIBLE, DISEASE FREE, WHICH IS WHY WE HAD TO HAVE SUCH A
STRICT MEDICAL BEFORE WE WENT. NO ONE HERE GETS TRAVELLERS
TUMMY. AS THE BUS ROLLED ALONG TOWARDS THE EQUATOR OF THE
SPHERE, THE FEELING OF GRAVITY BEGAN TO BUILD UP,TO NORMAL.
     YOUVE SEEN TELECASTS FROM INSIDE THE SPHERE, BUT THEY
DONT CONVEY THE ATMOSPHERE OF ACTUALLY BEING HERE. THE
CLIMATE IS TROPICAL LIKE THAT OF HAWAII, CONTROLLED BY THE
AMOUNT OF SUNLIGHT THEY LET IN EACH DAY. THE LIGHT IS
CAREFULLY FILTERED SO WE CAN GET A TAN WITHOUT SUNBURN.
SUNLIGHT PROVIDES ALL THE ELECTRICAL POWER FOR SKYWORLD,
TOO. AIR CONDITIONING UNITS KEEP THE AIR FRESH AND CLEAN,
LIKE IN AN ENORMOUS SUBMARINE. THEY SAY THAT IN LARGER
SKYWORLDS NEXT CENTURY THERE WILL EVEN BE CLOUDS AND RAINFALL.

THOUSANDS OF PEOPLE LIVE IN THE SPHERE, BUT IT DOESNT FEEL
CROWDED. LOOKING OUT OF THE HOTEL WINDOW, I CAN SEE THE
GROUND CURVING UPWARDS IN ALL DIRECTIONS. THE ODDEST THING
IS TO LOOK UP AND SEE PEOPLE ON THE OPPOSITE SIDE OF THE
SPHERE WITH THEIR HEADS POINTED TOWARDS YOU% THEY APPEAR
TO BE HANGING UPSIDE DOWN, BUT FROM THEIR POINT OF VIEW
THEYRE THE RIGHT WAY UP AND ITS YOU WHO ARE UPSIDE DOWN.
ITS DIFFICULT TO GET USED TO THE FEELING THAT SOMEONE IS
ALWAYS LOOKING DOWN ON YOU, BUT WHOEVER DESIGNED SKYWORLD
DID A GOOD JOB IN PROVIDING LOTS OF COVERED ALCOVES WHERE
YOU CAN SIT OR LIE IN PRIVACY.

THE ACOUSTICS INSIDE SKYWORLD ARE RATHER EERIE. THE WHOLE
SPHERE ECHOES SLIGHTLY, LIKE A LARGE EXHIBITION HALL, AND
SOMETIMES YOU CAN HEAR VOICES OF PEOPLE ON THE OPPOSITE
SIDE OF THE SPHERE AS THOUGH THEY WERE STANDING CLOSE TO
YOU.

I WOULDNT HAVE BELIEVED THAT THE SOIL LINING THE SPHERE IS
ACTUALLY IMPORTED MOON DUST - IT LOOKS LIKE DARK SAND.
ITS PARTICULARLY GOOD FOR GROWING THINGS IN. THE GRASS
AND TREES IN THE PARKS ARE FLOURISHING, BUT I WISH THERE
WERE MORE BIRDS AND ANIMALS HERE. APPARENTLY, DESIGNING A
SUCCESSFUL CLOSED ECOLOGY WAS MORE DIFFICULT THAN BUILDING
THE SPHERE ITSELF%

ALL THE BUILDINGS ARE MADE OF A RATHER DRAB DARK-GREY POROUS
BRICK WHICH IS ACTUALLY MOON ROCK MELTED AND CAST. BUT
THERES LOTS OF STAINED GLASS, ALSO MADE FROM MOON ROCK, TO
ADD COLOUR.

WE WERE ADVISED NOT TO MOVE AROUND TOO QUICKLY FOR THE
FIRST FEW DAYS, BECAUSE THE SLIGHT ROTATION OF THE COLONY
CAN MAKE YOU GIDDY AT FIRST. BUT WE WERE EAGER TO TRY THE
RECREATION ACTIVITIES AT THE AXIS OF THE SPHERE. AS YOU WALK
AROUND THE INSIDE OF THE SPHERE TOWARDS THE POLES YOU FEEL
     %%% LIGHTER. AT THE AXIS OF THE SPHERE ITSELF THERE IS NO
ROTATION AT ALL AND HENCE NO ARTIFICIAL GRAVITY.

JOHN HIRED A PEDALCOPTER AND FLEW OUT INTO THE MIDDLE OF
THE SPHERE UNDER HIS OWN POWER. ITS JUST LIKE SITTING ON
A BICYCLE= AS YOU PEDAL, THE WINGS FLAP, AND BEING WEIGHTLESS
YOU CAN EASILY FLY AROUND. THOSE EARLY AVIATION PIONEERS
WHO DREAMED OF FLYING LIKE BIRDS WOULD LOVE IT HERE. THIS
FORM OF WEIGHTLESS HUMAN-POWERERD FLIGHT DOES HAVE ITS
PROBLEMS, THOUGH. THE OTHER DAY SOMEONES PEDALCOPTER
BROKE DOWN AND THEY WERE STRANDED IN THE MIDDLE OF THE
SPHERE UNTIL SOMEONE CAME OUT TO RESCUE THEM.

I HEADED FOR THE CYLINDRICAL SWIMMING POOL AROUND SKYWORLDS
AXIS. THERES JUST ENOUGH ARTIFICIAL GRAVITY TO KEEP THE
WATER STUCK TO THE INSIDE OF THE CYLINDRICAL POOL, BUT IF
YOU JUMP HARD ENOUGH YOU CAN ACTUALLY DIVE UPWARDS INTO THE
WATER ABOVE YOUR HEAD%

TONIGHT WERE GOING TO A PARTY WHERE WE CAN SAMPLE   %%
CHATEAU SKYWORLD - WINE MADE FROM GRAPES GROWN IN THE
COLONYS OWN VINEYARDS.

HOPE ALL IS WELL WITH YOU. WELL HAVE LOTS OF 3-D HOLOSNAPS
TO SHOW YOU WHEN WE GET BACK.

LOVE

JILLY AND JOHN

   %%%

SKYONE

SW24.03.297

new worlds like the Earth. Few of those who build the first starships next century will live to see the pictures they send back, but it will be a wondrous legacy to leave their children.

From the foregoing it should be clear that voyaging between the stars is not going to be easy. It is natural to look for better energy sources than nuclear fusion. The ultimate source of energy is reactions between matter and antimatter. When matter and antimatter meet they annihilate each other to produce energy. This process is 100 per cent efficient, turning all the fuel into energy – hydrogen fusion is less than one per cent efficient at turning mass into energy. So does this energy source, the very best we can envisage, make feasible voyages like those of Captain Kirk in the starship Enterprise, assuming we can shield the ship against impacts from inter-stellar particles?

Calculations of the amount of energy required by a starship with a matter-antimatter drive to make a near-the-speed-of-light trip to a nearby star and back again show that it would need to carry 40,000 times its own weight in fuel.

The only way to bring fuel requirements down to realistic levels is to go more slowly. But then we are back where we started, for that rules out round trips to the stars in a human lifetime, unless we discover some radically new propulsion device such as the mythical warp drive beloved of science fiction writers. In short, high-speed trips to the stars take too much energy; and if we use less energy it takes too much time. The Universe is a big place and we must face up to the fact.

Breakthroughs in physics may one day make these calculations seem laughably old-fashioned. But in the meantime, if we are willing to work within the limits imposed by the Universe there is still much that can be done. And that includes colonizing the stars. For instance, we could hook up a Daedalus-type propulsion unit to a space colony and push it out towards the stars, like a space ark of science fiction. Journey time is not a constraint for a space ark, because new generations of occupants would be born en route. And because it's a one-way trip, fuel requirements are much reduced.

A space ark trip to Alpha Centauri might take 400 years, to Barnard's star 600 years, and to Tau Ceti 1,100 years. Once the colonists arrived at their destination they would set about building new habitats from raw materials around the star – once you are accustomed to living in a space colony, you do not need a habitable planet at your destination. In time, the colonists would launch a new wave of explorers to another destination, and so on until human life was spread throughout the Galaxy – or until it encountered someone else bent on similar schemes.

But why send people at all? Machines can explore the entire Galaxy on our behalf far more quickly and cheaply than a human expedition, and they will not be deterred by the most hostile of environments. Computers of unsurpassed cleverness will be the brains of starships. Daedalus, for example, will be too far away from Earth to request instructions from its makers once it encounters Barnard's star. It must make its own decisions as it goes along. Most interstellar exploration will be done by intelligent machines, not by living creatures.

Now think what an intelligent probe capable of reproducing itself could do. Programmed with instructions to make an identical twin of itself when it reached another star, it would set to work to dismantle an asteroid, build a new probe, and send it off to a new destination. Now there are two. Then three. And four. And so on.

Self-replicating machines are perfectly plausible in theory, and it will not be long before we see them in the factories of Earth. Admittedly, a starship reproducing itself in an alien solar system is a considerably more complex prospect than an industrial robot building a copy of itself on Earth, but the principle is sound. A few centuries from now, the first self-reproducing probe might be on its way to a nearby star.

Once we let a self-replicating probe loose on the Galaxy, there will be no stopping it, or its descendants. From then on, it is only a matter of time before every star has been visited by a probe, without any further effort on our part. All we have to do is to sit back and await the incoming flood of data.

Chapter Seven

LIFE IN THE SOLAR SYSTEM

So far we have concentrated on human life off Earth – the achievements of mankind in space travel and the prospects for the future. But what of the existence of other forms of life off Earth? Out there is a vast Universe, well stocked with the ingredients of life. How inconceivable it seems that our tiny planet should be the only place on which the seeds of life have taken root. The Universe offers near-endless possibilities for lifeforms to arise and develop. What might we find out there – and where will we find it?

A natural place to start is with the planets of our own solar system. Of the eight planets in addition to the Earth, only one or two are worth serious consideration as homes for life. Mercury and Venus can be quickly ruled out. Mercury, the closest planet to the Sun, is a small, rocky body only 50 per cent larger than our Moon. Like the Moon, it is airless, waterless, and is bathed in intense solar radiation.

Venus at first sight seems more promising, but it is nonetheless barren. Venus is almost the same size as the Earth; it has a dense atmosphere topped by unbroken clouds which veil the surface. Until the 1960s science fiction writers could hold out hope of Earth-like conditions on the planet, but scientific investigations have changed all that. Space probes have found that at the surface of the planet the temperature is a furnace-like 475°C, and the atmospheric pressure is 90 times that on the Earth. What is more, the atmosphere is almost entirely carbon dioxide, unbreathable to humans. Venus has virtually no water, which is essential to life as we know it. The clouds are made of corrosive sulphuric acid. Temperatures and pressures become more Earthlike higher in the atmosphere, but up there a deadly mist of sulphuric acid falls from the clouds. Venus is as hostile to life as any planet we could imagine.

Mars is an altogether more appealing world. It is half the size of the Earth but spins on its axis in only slightly more than 24 hours, so that the length of the day there would seem very familiar. Through a telescope it appears as a reddish-orange ball with white polar caps and dusky markings which might be mistaken for seas but for the fact that the Sun is never seen to reflect off them. Mars has a thin atmosphere in which high-speed winds whip up occasional sandstorms. The planet is a world of cold deserts.

For centuries, people have been willing to believe in the existence of life on Mars. As early as 1688 the Frenchman Bernard de Fontenelle, for no apparently good reason, speculated on the possibility of luminous birds on the planet (he seemed to be under the impression that similar birds existed in America). In 1938, a radio dramatization of the H. G. Wells novel *War of the Worlds* created hysteria in the United States among

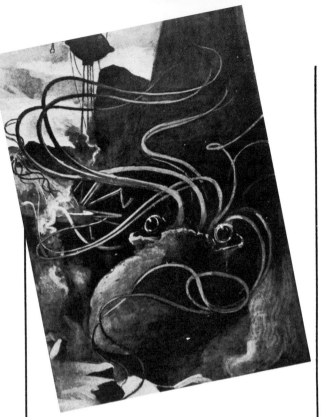

The terrible war machines of H. G. Wells's War of the Worlds may frighten no-one on paper but they frightened a lot of Americans on the radio in 1938.

listeners who became convinced that the world really was being invaded by rampaging Martians. In Minneapolis, a woman ran into a church, shouting: 'This is the end of the world. You might as well go home to die.' In Newark, New Jersey, families fled from their apartments with wet handkerchiefs and towels over their faces to protect themselves from what they believed was a Martian gas attack. A man in Pittsburgh found his wife clutching a bottle of poison, screaming: 'I'd rather die this way.' All over the nation, citizens huddled in churches to pray, made tearful farewell phone calls to distant relatives, and jammed the switchboards of police, newspapers, and radio stations.

The story of life on Mars really started in 1877 when the Italian astronomer Giovanni Schiaparelli observed what he described as 'a network of numerous lines or fine stripes' criss-crossing the planet's red deserts. He termed them *canali*, a word which strictly means channels but which most people took to mean canals, with the attendant implication that they were artificial.

Schiaparelli never insisted they were artificial, but for an American astronomer, Percival Lowell, there was no doubt. Lowell pictured a Martian civilization engaged in a life-or-death struggle against drought. The canal network, he asserted, was to bring water from the polar caps to the Martians' crops at the equator – those dark areas, which Lowell said were extensive agricultural plantations.

The Mars of science fiction, including *War of the Worlds*, is the Mars of Percival Lowell. Alas, it bears no relation to the real Mars. Even in Lowell's time there was fierce opposition to his speculations. In 1907 Alfred Russel Wallace, a colleague of Charles Darwin, appreciated that Mars was too cold and dry for advanced life, and he stated flatly that the planet was both uninhabited and uninhabitable. As observers looked at Mars more carefully with bigger and better telescopes, they reported that the canals were not fine, straight lines at all, but actually disconnected dots and splotches. The canals were an optical illusion, a product of the human eye and brain, not of Martian civilization.

Astronomer Percival Lowell was so convinced that the criss-cross stripes he saw through his telescope were canals bringing water from polar ice caps to drought-ridden Martians, that he drew a map of the planet complete with names.

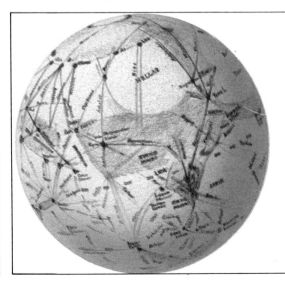

This did not rule out the possibility that some lowly form of vegetation might exist on the surface. But the possibility of moss or lichen on Mars could hardly compete in the popular imagination with the novels of Edgar Rice Burroughs in which hero John Carter roamed a world of beautiful princesses, eight-legged beasts and a widespread network of irrigation canals, complete with pumping stations. Faced with such romantic speculations, who wanted to know that there was no liquid water on Mars, or that the air was too thin to breathe?

As spacecraft began to expand our view of Mars, hopes of finding even lowly life on the planet seemed to fade. Mariner 4 in 1965 sent back the first pictures which revealed Mars to be cratered like the Moon, an impression reinforced in 1969 by Mariners 6 and 7. Measurements of the atmosphere of Mars showed that it was made primarily of carbon dioxide at a pressure less than one per cent that of the Earth's atmosphere, even lower than expected. With such little air cover the surface of Mars must suffer permanent sub-zero temperatures everywhere, with no protection from the Sun's ultra-violet radiation.

Space probes have shown that Lowell's canals do not exist. This globe of Mars was made from photographs taken by Mariner 9. In place of Lowell's canals were found vast canyons and towering volcanoes. Of life there was no sign.

Better news came from Mariner 9 in 1971 which spotted important features that the previous probes had missed: enormous volcanoes and apparent dried-up river beds. Perhaps in the past the volcanoes had erupted volumes of gas, giving Mars a temporary atmosphere dense enough to support liquid water – and perhaps life. The only way to find out for sure was to go down and look. That was the job of the two Viking probes which landed on Mars in 1976.

At each of their landing sites, the Viking probes cautiously opened their TV eyes and looked around. They saw a rock-strewn landscape similar to the desert areas of Arizona, Peru, or southwest Egypt. Of a cactus or even a tuft of grass, still less a camel, there was no sign. Viking's cameras were good enough to detect small creatures hopping or burrowing in the soil, had there been any. Some people have speculated that life on other planets might be based on silicon, rather than on carbon as on Earth. In that case, the lifeform might resemble a rock, for silicon is the main constituent of rocks. There are plenty of rocks on Mars. Viking lander pictures taken over a period of months have been carefully compared – but none of the rocks has moved . . .

The Vikings also carried miniature biology laboratories to automatically analyse samples of the soil for microscopic organisms – little green bugs – that might live unseen in the red sands. Handfuls of soil were collected by a scoop and incubated in three different ways in an attempt to make Martian bugs grow.

First, the so-called 'chicken soup' experiment fed a sample of Mars soil with a rich broth – the 'chicken soup'. Any Martian organisms in the soil would, it was hoped, eat the soup, causing the bugs to grow and reproduce, giving off gases in the process that could be detected by Viking's equipment. When the nutrient was added to the sample, carbon dioxide and oxygen gushed from it. Was this the first startling evidence of life on Mars? Alas, the gas emissions had a more mundane cause: simple chemical reactions between the liquid nutrient and the very dry, highly oxidized Martian soil. Such reactions may be useful one day if we wish to create a denser atmosphere on Mars, but they provide no evidence for the existence of Martian life. Experiment one had drawn a blank.

Experiment two looked for evidence of plant cells in the Martian soil. If such cells existed, they might take up carbon from the atmosphere by the process known as photosynthesis, as do plants on Earth. So a sample of Martian soil was incubated under an atmosphere of carbon dioxide and carbon monoxide gas. After the incubation period, analysis of the soil showed that small amounts of carbon had indeed been taken up from the atmosphere, just as though a scattering of plantlike organisms were living in the Martian soil. To check this, another sample was sterilized by heating before incubation to kill any organisms that might be in it; hence in this sample there should have been no uptake of carbon from the simulated atmosphere. But the result was the same as before. Again, biologists concluded that it must be chemical reactions that were responsible for the uptake of carbon, not Martian life. Experiment two also had drawn a blank.

Experiment three worked the opposite way to experiment two. It took a sample of Mars soil and added a nutrient containing carbon. Bugs in the soil might be expected to release gases containing carbon, which the experiment was designed to detect. And when the experiment was tried out with a sample of Mars soil, some of the carbon was indeed given off. A second sample, heat sterilized before incubation, gave off no carbon, exactly as would be expected if life were responsible for the carbon emission. So had Viking found what it came for? Not necessarily. Chemical reactions similar to those which produced the gas emissions of experiment one could still be responsible. A possible explanation was that carbon in the nutrient was joining with oxygen in the soil, giving rise to carbon dioxide gas which Viking detected. So this third experiment turned out to be tantalizingly ambiguous.

To assess the Viking biology experiments properly, we must also take into account the results from a related instrument which analysed the Martian soil in search of organic molecules that might make up the bodies of Martian organisms. Even if Martian life were based on some totally alien biochemistry, this sophisticated instrument, called a gas chromatograph mass spectrometer, should still have detected it. But this instrument found only carbon dioxide and oxygen in the soil, with no sign of the complex molecules that exist in meteorites or the gas clouds of space. This negative result has led most scientists to conclude that life does not exist on Mars.

However, biologists Gilbert Levin and Patricia Straat, originators of the third Viking experiment, have spent 3½ years trying to duplicate the observed carbon emission using simulated Martian soils, without success. Their failure does not necessarily mean that chemical explanations are ruled out; we do not fully understand the nature of the Martian surface, so the simulated soils may not be fully accurate. Alone among the Viking experimenters, Levin and Straat have continued to argue that their experiment may have detected biological activity on Mars.

To support their case, they note that certain terrestrial microbes including lichens, algae, fungi, and bacteria are known to survive Mars-like conditions. Yellow-green patches on some rocks near the Viking 1 lander changed in colour and shape with time. These changes could be due to the effects of wind-blown dust, tricks of the light, or artefacts of Viking's cameras. But, suggest Levin and Straat, it just might be evidence of lichen patches on the rocks of Mars.

Evidence of how pervasive life can be, at least on the Earth, has come from the so-called dry valleys of Antarctica. These are snow-free regions swept by bitter winds. The combination of cold and dryness makes them as close to conditions on Mars as anything on Earth can be. The dry valleys of Antarctica had long been thought to be lifeless – but a few years ago when scientists broke open some rocks they found under the surface a dark greenish layer of microbes a few millimetres thick. By living within rocks, or in pores or fissures between rocks, the organisms find an environment that is warmer and more protected than on the surface. Is this where the life is on Mars?

Not everyone is convinced. For one thing, it is worrying that no organic molecules of any

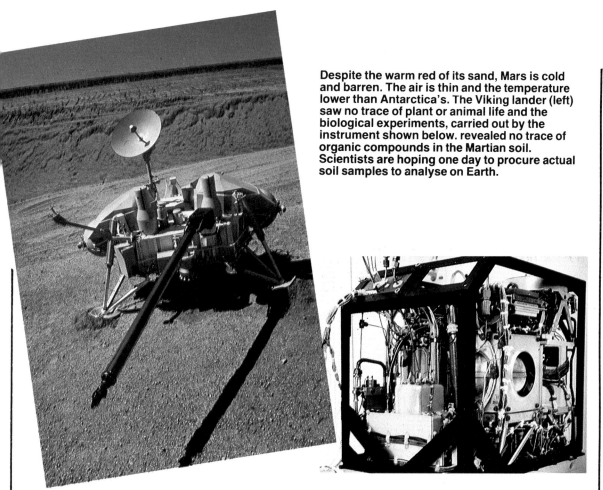

Despite the warm red of its sand, Mars is cold and barren. The air is thin and the temperature lower than Antarctica's. The Viking lander (left) saw no trace of plant or animal life and the biological experiments, carried out by the instrument shown below. revealed no trace of organic compounds in the Martian soil. Scientists are hoping one day to procure actual soil samples to analyse on Earth.

sort were detected in the soil of Mars, when at least a smattering would be expected from the carbon-containing meteorites that land on the planet. Even though Viking looked under a rock, a sheltered and hence favourable location for life, it did not find any organic matter. Evidently any organic molecules that reach the surface of Mars must soon be destroyed. How this happens has been demonstrated by a team of scientists led by Kevin Pang of NASA's Jet Propulsion Laboratory.

They exposed a sample of carbon-containing meteorite to simulated Martian conditions. Under the Sun's ultraviolet light, the organic molecules in the meteorite combined with a trace of oxygen in the Martian air to form carbon dioxide and other simple gases. Similarly, any living thing exposed at the Martian surface would be broken down into gases by the Sun's ultraviolet radiation.

Some biologists have suggested that life on Mars exists in certain favoured oases, such as around the polar caps where water is more plentiful. NASA has plans for sending automatic rovers to Mars which would roam the surface of Mars in search of life. At present NASA cannot get the money to send them, but according to Pang and his colleagues that does not matter because there is no life there to be found anyway. All latitudes on Mars receive a lethal dose of solar ultraviolet radiation, they say.

A sensitive technique in analysing a substance for the presence of organic matter is to measure the way in which it reflects ultraviolet and infra-red radiation. Scans of Mars by spacecraft and through telescopes from Earth have drawn a blank, even though a trace of organic molecules as small as that in meteorites (one-tenth of one per cent) would have shown up in these observations.

There is one other simple observation that argues strongly against the existence of life on Mars, and that concerns the composition of its atmosphere. On Earth, the atmosphere contains a large amount of oxygen and smaller amounts of methane, both produced by life. On Mars, by contrast, there is only a trace of oxygen and no detectable methane; the atmosphere of Mars would be markedly different if there were life on the planet. Therefore we must reluctantly conclude that the sterility of the Viking landing sites is typical of Mars as a whole.

Of the other planets, Jupiter is the only one that seems a possible home for life. Jupiter might at first sound an unlikely prospect, for it is a ball of gas with no solid surface. But some sort of airborne life might float among its clouds – not birds or insects but creatures that have more in common with life in the seas of Earth. A few years ago, Carl Sagan and Edwin Salpeter of Cornell University imagined a three-tier hierarchy of lifeforms for the Jovian atmosphere. At the start of the food chain are the equivalent of plankton – small organisms Sagan and Salpeter term sinkers, which rain down from the upper levels of Jupiter's clouds to provide food for larger organisms, the equivalent of fish, hovering deeper in the atmosphere – call them floaters. In turn, the floaters are preyed upon by the largest organisms of all, the equivalent of sharks or whales, called hunters. Floaters and hunters are balloon-like organisms buoyed up by helium gas. They choose their favoured level in the clouds by altering their internal pressure, and move around by expelling jets of helium.

Jupiter's atmosphere, similar in composition to interstellar clouds, is probably a sample of the cloud from which the Sun and planets grew, complete with its rich mixture of organic chemicals. The palette of red, yellow, and brown colours that splashes the clouds of Jupiter is probably based on complex organic molecules. Close-up views of Jupiter taken by the Voyager space probes in 1979 show the atmosphere to be whipped up by swirling storms and turbulent convection cells. In view of this, it is difficult to envisage how life could survive there, let alone have originated there. The Galileo probe, which is due in the late 1980s to plunge into Jupiter's atmosphere and analyse it, may tell us more about the chances of airborne life on Jupiter.

No planet beyond Jupiter holds out any better hope of finding life. But Jupiter and its smaller brother Saturn are surrounded by retinues of moons, which are worlds in their own right. Among the many and varied conditions on these worldlets, are some suitable for life? Saturn's largest moon, Titan, has always seemed the favourite, for it is the only moon known to possess a substantial atmosphere, and with a diameter larger than Mercury deserves consideration as an object of planetary status. The Voyager space probes found the atmosphere of Titan to consist mostly of nitrogen, the major constituent of our own atmosphere, with some methane. Titan's atmosphere is topped by an orange smog of hydrocarbons. We might learn something about the origin of life by studying the atmosphere of Titan, but we are unlikely to find life itself there. Titan's surface is so cold that a rain of liquid nitrogen falls into pools on a tarry surface. Titan is like a deep-freeze version of the primitive Earth.

There is one other possibility. Europa, a frozen moon of Jupiter slightly smaller than our own Moon, has been identified as the most likely home for life off Earth in the solar system by Richard Hoagland, an American science writer and consultant to NASA. Europa's icy crust is cracked in places, like the surface of a frozen pond. Through the cracks seems to be oozing some dark, brownish substance. Could these be tarry organic molecules? And could there exist oceans under the ice, possibly containing life?

When Jupiter formed it would have glowed like a small star from the heat of its contraction. Europa could then have been covered with an ocean of liquid water, one of the prime requisites for life, missing on all planets other than the Earth. Drawing energy from the warmth of Jupiter, organic molecules in that deep, warm ocean of Europa may have formed themselves into some kind of life – only to find themselves trapped as Jupiter cooled and Europa froze over. Europa's seas remain liquid under the ice because of the heat released by tides that are raised on Europa by Jupiter's gravity.

In Hoagland's view, the ocean of Europa

might teem with shoals of marine life similar to that which exists in the deep oceans of Earth where sunlight never penetrates. Our first expedition to look for life on Europa might have as much in common with a deep-sea diving exploit as a space mission. Were we to break the crust of Europa, might we find the equivalent of plesiosaurs swimming there, or of dolphins or some other creatures, locked under the ice and knowing nothing beyond their dark liquid world?

All this speculation assumes, of course, that life will arise spontaneously wherever conditions are right, as it is presumed to have done nearly 4,000 million years ago on Earth. As yet, no one knows how life arose on Earth. Biologists Francis Crick and Leslie Orgel have sidestepped the whole problem by suggesting that life was deliberately seeded here in the form of bacteria which arrived in an automatic space probe sent by some alien civilization. In other words, they claim that the Earth has been terraformed – but by extra-terrestrials.

Bacteria are a good way of transferring life over long distances. They can remain frozen indefinitely, enabling them to withstand interstellar trips, and being so small billions of them can be packed into a matchbox. If several dozen parcels of bacteria were dropped onto a young planet by a visiting spaceship, some should land in a suitable warm pool where they could flourish – and eventually move out to cover the planet. In this way, a determined civilization could seed the entire Galaxy, as we may one day do.

Fascinating though this theory is, it does not solve the question of the origin of life, but merely displaces it. Most scientists subscribe to the view that life arose from the mixture of gases that surrounded the primitive Earth. But exactly what those gases were remains uncertain. Until a few years ago it was generally believed that the atmosphere of the early Earth was similar to that of present-day Jupi-

It is too soon to rule out the possibility of life on Jupiter although the Voyager probe's observation of its turbulent surface makes it seem unlikely. Some scientists now pin their hopes on Jupiter's moon Europa (below) where deep, warm oceans may conceal advanced life-forms.

ter, with large amounts of hydrogen, ammonia, methane, and water vapour. Experiments conducted in 1953 by the American chemists Stanley Miller and Harold Urey demonstrated that such a gas mixture, when subjected to an energy source, gives rise to complex organic molecules known as amino acids, which are the building blocks of protein. The energy sources required for this transition can be any of those occurring readily in nature: lightning strokes, sunlight,

In his story A Meeting with Medusa, Arthur C. Clarke depicts an ocean world where giant stinging jellyfish – the medusae – fight life and death battles with lethal electric rays – the mantas.

shock waves from meteorite impacts or thunderclaps, and heat from volcanoes.

Unfortunately, geological evidence from ancient rocks has made it clear that the composition of the early Earth's atmosphere was not like this at all; the main gases were probably carbon dioxide, water vapour, nitrogen, and carbon monoxide. These are the gases which are erupted most abundantly from the interior of the Earth through volcanoes. Geologists believe that, over geological time, the Earth's oceans and atmosphere would have built up from the products of volcanic eruptions. Experiments suggest that, as long as small amounts of methane and ammonia were mixed in with these gases, the

molecules of life could have arisen by the processes first demonstrated by Miller and Urey.

Actual living cells could, it is supposed, build up from these molecules in and around the seas of Earth, though at present no one has any clear idea of exactly how this great step forward was taken. Whatever the origin of life, we know from geological evidence that the first living cells existed on Earth over 3,000 million years ago. For three quarters of its existence our planet has supported life. The processes of life, in particular the action of plants in breaking down carbon dioxide to produce free oxygen, have modified the atmosphere into its present-day composition.

A radical alternative to this conventional view of the origin of life has been proposed by Professors Fred Hoyle and Chandra Wickramasinghe of University College, Cardiff. According to their revolutionary theory, living cells form in the rich chemical stew of interstellar clouds and are seeded onto planets by passing comets. If this theory were true it could mean that terrestrial-type life is widespread throughout the Galaxy.

Hoyle and Wickramasinghe argue that the new-born Earth did not have an atmosphere, and therefore could not have been the site of the origin of life. They believe instead that the Earth was originally a dry, airless ball

similar to our present-day Moon, and that the gases of its atmosphere and the waters of the oceans were introduced from space by the arrival of comets from the outer reaches of the solar system. Once the Earth had developed an atmosphere by this process, the blanket of gases would have cushioned the impact of further comets which brought life to our planet from space.

In contradiction of this theory, there is good geological evidence that the Earth's atmosphere was exhaled from its interior through the mouths of volcanoes, as mentioned above; on the other hand, it is probable that many comets did strike the Earth early in its history. Perhaps there is something to be said for both sides of the argument. But the most controversial part of the theory concerns the origin of life in comets. Hoyle and Wickramasinghe propose that life built up on the surfaces and in the interiors of comets as the comets shuttled through the rich cloud of chemicals surrounding the Sun at its birth. The chemically rich, water-bearing interior of a comet is the most likely site for the emergence of the first living cells, they assert. Some of these living cells would be delivered to the surfaces of planets while others would be returned to the gas cloud. Still other cells would remain dormant inside comets until the present day.

In this theory, the complex organic molecules observed in interstellar clouds are actually remnants of living cells that have been expelled from comets. To support their case, Hoyle and Wickramasinghe have presented observations which, they say, reveal the existence of cellulose in interstellar clouds. Cellulose is the most abundant organic substance on Earth, forming the cell walls of plants and trees. The observations, which concern the way in which dust in interstellar clouds absorbs light at infra-red wavelengths, are also claimed to show the presence of other important biochemicals such as starch.

But the interpretation of these observations has been questioned, notably by Carl Sagan and his colleague Bishun Khare of Cornell University. Sagan and Khare conclude that the observations indicate the existence of nothing more spectacular than a dark brownish solid which they term 'star tar'. This tarry substance is produced in experiments like those first carried out by Miller and Urey. Sagan and Khare believe that star tar is distributed in the form of tiny grains like smoke particles throughout interstellar clouds. Star tar, they say, can account for the infra-red observations better than can cellulose, starch, or living cells.

If Hoyle and Wickramasinghe's speculations are correct, there should be confirmatory evidence close at hand – in the comets of our own solar system. We do not even need to send a space probe to search for life in a comet, because Hoyle and Wickramasinghe claim that the Earth is regularly invaded by comet-borne organisms which grow within our bodies. This sounds rather like the science-fiction film *Alien*, except that in this case the alien lifeforms invading our bodies are not huge monsters but bacteria and viruses which cause disease.

In this bizarre extension of their life-from-space theory, Hoyle and Wickramasinghe postulate that living cells reach the Earth when our planet passes through swarms of cometary dust, as frequently happens. These organisms float down through the atmosphere to the ground, where they are inhaled or ingested to produce illness, notably colds and flu but also more dangerous epidemics such as measles, smallpox, and plague. In other words, the cold you had last winter came from space, by the same process that originally brought life to Earth four billion years ago.

Hoyle and Wickramasinghe note that the famous Asian flu epidemic of 1957 and the so-called Hong Kong flu of 1968 had certain similarities with flu outbreaks of 77 and 78 years previously. They therefore suggest that both these forms of flu came from Halley's comet, whose orbital period has varied over the past two millenia from 75 to 79 years. If diseases really do come from space, this is powerful evidence in favour of Hoyle and Wickramasinghe's theory for the origin of life.

One possible objection is that cometary dust is swept up by other bodies in space, not just the Earth; so why have we not found any sign

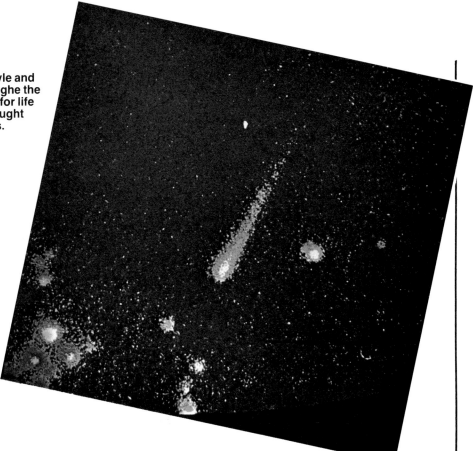

According to Fred Hoyle and Chandra Wickramasinghe the conditions necessary for life and life itself were brought to the Earth by comets. Even today 'germs' producing epidemics of flu and worse diseases are rained on us with cometary dust, they say. There is, however, no evidence that comets such as Kohoutek (pictured here by Skylab in false colour in 1973) have brought diseases to Earth.

of such life in Moon rocks or on Mars? The reason, say the two scientists, is that the organisms would be so thinly spread that they would escape detection. Humans are actually highly sensitive detectors of influenza viruses. Only a few influenza virus particles are needed for a person to become infected; no laboratory detector could compare with the response of a human to a virus.

Hoyle and Wickramasinghe's heretical ideas about diseases from space have caused a storm of protest from the medical community and from fellow astronomers. One clear weakness of the theory is that there is no demonstrated link between the occurrence of disease and the influx of yearly meteor showers, which are the densest concentrations of cometary dust that the Earth encounters. In particular, two meteor showers – the Eta Aquarids which occur each May and the Orionids of October – are both believed to be debris from Halley's comet, the very comet which Hoyle and Wickramasinghe identify as the carrier of influenza. So if the theory were correct one would expect to find outbreaks of flu peaking yearly after these meteor showers, but they do not.

Hoyle and Wickramasinghe's theory is exciting because it implies that life will form easily and will be found on any suitable planets throughout the Galaxy, as well as in comets and meteorites orbiting the Sun and other stars. Alas, though, the balance of evidence seems strongly against the theory. Perhaps only a sample-return mission to a comet will provide the final answer, but no such mission is planned for the foreseeable future. Maybe one day a meteorite will land bearing living cells of extraterrestrial origin, formed from the gas cloud that once surrounded the Sun. Then we will know.

Otherwise, it seems we must stick to the conventional view that life arose spontaneously on Earth, and we are thus no nearer to knowing whether life on Earth is a freak or whether similar conditions have been repeated on endless worlds around other stars.

Chapter Eight

LIFE AMONG THE STARS

A re there other civilizations in space, and if so how many? Such a question may seem utterly unfathomable. Yet there exists a formulation that allows us to make some rational assessment of the probability of extraterrestrial life. It is called the Drake formula, after the American radio astronomer Frank Drake who first expressed it in 1961.

Briefly, the formula asserts that the number of civilizations in space is governed by a magical seven factors: the average rate of star formation in the Galaxy; the fraction of stars with planets; the number of planets in each solar system suitable for life; the percentage of planets in each system on which life actually arises; the likelihood of life becoming intelligent; the desire of that intelligent life-form to communicate; and, finally, the average longevity of such civilizations, including our own. Multiply together these factors and you have calculated the number of civilizations in our Galaxy today. It is exceedingly simple in theory, but in practice it is a formula with no clear solution.

The first factor is easy to determine. There are approximately 100,000 million stars in the Galaxy, and the Galaxy is roughly 10,000 million years old; therefore on average 10 stars have been formed per year. The remaining factors are increasingly speculative, making the outcome of the Drake formula correspondingly uncertain. Different ·scientists have offered various values for each factor,

resulting in final estimates ranging from as many as 100 million civilizations in the Galaxy down to a lower limit of just one – ourselves. In the 1960s, astronomers tended to make estimates towards the high end of this range but, as we shall see, a persuasive new movement has arisen which argues that the true figure lies at the bottom of the scale.

One of the most fascinating unknowns in the Drake formula, and one which astronomers are making real progress to resolve, concerns the existence of planetary systems around other stars. Without planets, there can be no life as we know it. At present, astronomers do not have firm evidence for any planetary system other than our own. The problem is that planets of other stars are too faint to be seen directly through telescopes on Earth. For instance, an observer at Alpha Centauri would not be able to see our largest planet, Jupiter, because the glare from the Sun, 2,000 million times brighter, would swamp its faint light. Large telescopes in space, above the blurring effect of the Earth's turbulent atmosphere, might just catch a glimpse of large planets going round other stars, but the chances seem slim. Astronomers have therefore turned to indirect methods of detecting planets of other stars.

F ortunately, planets give their existence away by the slight effect they have on the motion of their parent stars. A star and planet can be thought of as two very unequal ends of

By studying the 'wobble' of stars, scientists can detect the presence of orbiting planets.

a dumbbell, rotating around their common centre of gravity. The centre of gravity is much closer to the star than it is to the planet because the star is of course much heavier. But if the planet is big enough, the star seems to wobble slightly as the planet swings in orbit around it. The heavier the planet is, the further from the star the centre of gravity is, and hence the bigger the wobble it causes. The period of the wobble mirrors the orbital period of the planet, or planets. A small planet such as the Earth has such a tiny effect on the Sun that our parent star hardly moves at all as we orbit it, but large planets such as Jupiter and Saturn cause a wobble in the Sun's position that would be detectable by observers orbiting nearby stars.

Astronomers can detect the wobble of a star in two ways: either through its slight motion towards and away from us, or from its side-to-side shift in position. Information about the backwards-and-forwards motion of the star is found from analysis of the star's light. Light from a source that is moving towards or away from the Earth undergoes a shift in wavelength known as the Doppler shift. When a star approaches us, its light is shortened in wavelength; as it recedes, the light is lengthened in wavelength. These wavelength changes are measured by studying a spectrum of the star's light.

It is simple in theory, but the speeds involved are relatively slow, about 46 km/h for a Jupiter-mass planet orbiting a star like the Sun, which makes them difficult to measure. Existing methods for analysing the spectrum of light from stars and galaxies yield accuracies of about 3,200 km/h. So to detect the tell-tale wobble of stars caused by a planetary system requires a hundredfold increase in accuracy of measuring systems. Astronomers at the University of Arizona are developing equipment which they hope will reveal star motions as slow as 36 km/h or even better, sufficient to reveal the existence of Jupiter-sized planets around most of the stars in our neighbourhood.

The other method of searching for planets is already in use and has begun to produce tantalizing results. It involves plotting a star's position over many years to detect any side-to-side wobble caused as a planet orbits it. The star is photographed regularly and its position is measured with respect to background stars that do not move. Extreme precision is required. Any position shift caused by a planet would be very small; a planet like Jupiter orbiting even a lightweight nearby star would cause a wobble in the star's position equivalent to the apparent width of a human hair as seen from a distance of a few miles. But existing techniques are accurate enough to detect such tiny shifts.

An American astronomer, Peter van de Kamp, has been tracking the red dwarf Barnard's star, 6 light years away, for more than 40 years. He believes he has found a wobble in its motion that reveals the existence of two planets similar in size to Jupiter and Saturn orbiting the star every 12 and 20 years respectively. There may also be other planets too small to show up. If so, this would be exciting news, for Barnard's star is the second closest star to our Sun. But other astronomers dispute van de Kamp's results, saying that the microscopic wobble is caused by faults in his telescope or photographic plates.

To resolve the question, and to find even smaller wobbles of other stars, more sensitive equipment is needed. At Pittsburgh's Allegheny Observatory, Dr George Gatewood has devised a new technique for planet-hunting. Forsaking photographic plates, he has turned instead to electronic detectors. Bundles of fibre optics feed star images from the Observatory's 30-inch (76-centimetre) refracting telescope into photoelectric detectors which measure the relative positions of the stars with unprecedented precision. This device, called a Multichannel Astrometric Photometer (MAP) can measure a star's position in one night more accurately than in a year of observing with photographic plates. The MAP is sensitive enough to detect Jupiter-like planets around several hundred nearby stars.

Gatewood is currently examining three dozen nearby stars for planet-induced wobbles, a task which should produce firm conclusions within a decade. Astronomers of the 1990s should know for certain how common planetary systems are around stars. Meanwhile, it seems reasonable to estimate the fraction of stars with planets as one in ten.

Returning to the Drake formula, the next factor to be considered is the number of planets in each solar system that are suitable for life. Our own solar system certainly has one planet suitable for life (the Earth!) and it seems that Mars came close to being a life-bearing planet. So an average of one suitable planet per system seems a reasonable number to pick. But on how many of those planets will life actually come into existence? Scientists usually assume that life will arise on most planets where conditions are right and, given time, will in many cases evolve towards an intelligent, technological level similar to our own with a desire to make contact with its neighbours.

Putting estimates like these into the Drake formula yields the startling result that one new civilization like ours emerges in the Galaxy every 10 years. (Soberingly, one civilization also dies every 10 years). How many civilizations are there in all? That depends how long each one lasts. Some civilizations may rapidly wipe themselves out due to wars, famine, overpopulation, pollution, or other catastrophe. Others may survive for a long time but soon lose the desire to communicate, making them undetectable to us. The outcome of the Drake formula depends most strongly on the figure we choose for the average lifetime of high-tech civilizations. If it is a long time, such as 1,000 million years, then in combination with the figures assumed above we find that there are 100 million other civilizations out there. If the average lifetime is short, such as a century, then we are one of only about 10 civilizations at present, and the Galaxy is littered with the decaying remains of many failed civilizations. A favoured compromise figure for the average lifetime of civilizations is 10 million years, which means that there are one million civilizations for us to talk to, if we adopt the most popular values for the other factors in the Drake formula.

But is there some erroneous assumption or missing factor in the Drake formula that would invalidate these optimistic conclusions? Biologists argue that there are so many possible evolutionary pathways for life to follow that the chance of ending up with intelligent beings is extremely remote, and therefore we are effectively alone. Certainly, the evolutionary history that led to modern man would never be exactly repeated elsewhere; on the other hand, might there be many other routes which lead to approximately the same result? (We shall look at some possibilities later in this chapter.) The arguments over this biological question are impossible to resolve with our current state of knowledge, but it does seem that the relevant factor in the Drake formula concerning the emergence of intelligence should not be set too high.

A different reason for assuming that we are most likely alone has been presented by an American astronomer, Michael Hart. He proposes that the habitable temperate zone around stars is much narrower than previously supposed – so much so that the chances of getting the right type of planet at the right distance around the right sort of star are negligible.

Hart has performed computer simulations of the evolution of the Earth's atmospheric composition and surface temperature, taking into account various effects such as geological processes and the emergence of simple living organisms. He finds that if the Earth had been only about 5 per cent closer to the Sun than it is today, it would have suffered a so-called runaway greenhouse effect early in its history, turning it into a roasting inferno like Venus. Had the Earth's distance from the Sun been only about one per cent greater than it actually is, it would have suffered a runaway glaciation about 2,000 million years ago. In other words, the habitable zone around the Sun is no more than about 9 million kilometres wide.

But there is worse to come, because the habitable zone does not remain constant in location during the star's history. Stars slowly increase in luminosity as they grow older (our Sun has brightened by about 30 per cent over its lifetime), so the habitable zone moves gradually outwards with time. A planet is therefore faced with a tall order: it has to survive the cooler early stages of the star without freezing over, and the warmer later stages without roasting. To give sufficient time for intelligent life to arise, the progressively moving zone of habitability must overlap the planet's orbit for billions of years. This requirement limits the allowable orbits around a star so severely that it would not be surprising if the Earth were a rarity. Even our time may be up relatively soon, for according to the English physicist James

Lovelock the continued increase in the Sun's luminosity will start to make the Earth uninhabitably warm in 100 million years' time.

If high-tech civilizations are as abundant as the Drake formula predicts, we should expect to see some sign of them as a result of what might be termed the Columbus effect: advanced civilizations tend to seek out new worlds and primitive societies. Most, if not all civilizations like our own would want to explore other stars and any planetary systems they possess. The most economical way would be to do this with self-replicating probes of the type discussed at the end of Chapter 6.

Various computer studies have shown that a wave of colonization starting out from one inhabited planet anywhere in the Galaxy at about one-tenth the speed of light (the speed of the proposed Daedalus starship described in Chapter 6) will lead to the complete col-

The Multichannel Astrometric Photometer (MAP) can measure a star's position more accurately in one night than conventional photography can in one year. The instrument gathers light with bundles of fibre optics.

onization of the Galaxy within a few million years, assuming that each probe takes no longer than 1,000 years to reproduce itself when it reaches a star. Even if the speed of travel is restricted to that of present-day space probes such as the Voyagers, every star in the Galaxy will still have been visited in about 100 million years.

This may seem a long time, but it is short compared with the lifetimes of stars and planets, which are measured in thousands of millions of years; and it is only one per cent the age of the Galaxy. Once a fleet of such probes had been sent out, even the death of their parent civilization would not affect them. Therefore, if there are lots of high-tech civilizations in the Galaxy, and if the first of them arose more than about 100 million years ago, either they or their machines should already be in our solar system.

This astonishing conclusion is difficult to avoid. There may of course be many reasons why a civilization would not want to colonize the Galaxy – for instance, they might not be interested in space exploration; they might consider the distances or timescales too great;

or they are nomads who move on. But it is difficult to believe there are reasons which would exclude every civilization from mounting a colonization drive at some time in its existence. If only one of the many civilizations predicted by the Drake formula decides to send out self-replicating probes – as we ourselves may do in the next few centuries – then it is only a matter of time before every star in the Galaxy contains some evidence of that civilization's existence. So where are they?

There are three possible answers: either they are here and we see them in the form of flying saucers; or they are here but we have overlooked them or they are hiding; or they are not here at all, because we are the only high-tech civilization in the Galaxy, or at least one of the very first. All of these answers are startling. The first possibility is examined in more detail in Chapter 10, so it is sufficient to say here that most scientists reject the idea that UFOs are alien spacecraft, even those who believe strongly in the existence of extraterrestrial life. For one thing, an alien

probe in our solar system could most easily make contact with us by beaming a radio signal at us, as happened in the film *Close Encounters of the Third Kind*; but no such signals have been received.

Of course, if alien probes were here they might be programmed merely to observe and not to make contact. The most likely place to find them would be where raw materials are most plentiful, which is in the asteroid belt. Perhaps some of the asteroids are actually alien probes or space colonies. Intriguingly, astronomers believe that originally there were only a few large asteroids which have since been broken up by collisions to form the many thousands of fragments observed today. Is it possible that the large asteroids were actually broken up not by collisions but by mining activities of alien probes?

The final possibility, that we are alone after all, may seem unpalatable, but it has a growing number of adherents among scientists who have examined and rejected all other explanations for the lack of any sign of extraterrestrials. The conclusion that we are alone is certainly consistent with the available evidence. But to many astronomers this conclusion is too sweeping to make in our current state of ignorance. They argue that we should first search more carefully for evidence of extraterrestrials, as described in the next chapter.

Even if we are the most advanced technological civilization in the galaxy, that does not rule out the possibility of all sorts of fascinating life forms on other planets. Life off Earth will differ in many ways from the life with which we are familiar; that is one prediction we can make with confidence.

Alien lifeforms might not be based on the same chemicals as ourselves. For instance, ammonia could replace water as a solvent, particularly on colder planets and on those with higher atmospheric pressures than

On a high gravity 'heavy' planet upright creatures would find movement difficult. Ground-hugging life-forms, perhaps resembling the sandsharks envisaged by Dougal Dixon, might evolve.

Earth – ammonia is a liquid only at sub-zero temperatures under normal atmospheric pressure, but its boiling point goes up as the pressure is raised. In our own solar system Jupiter and Saturn provide the best locations for ammonia-based life, but it is possible to imagine an Earth-sized world with seas of ammonia (Saturn's moon Titan almost qualifies as such a world). If ammonia lifeforms are possible, the traditional concept of habitable zones around stars will have to be extended. Other suggested solvents include carbon dioxide, which is another low-temperature, high-pressure liquid that might be found on a Venus-like planet far from its parent star; and methyl alcohol (the sort of alcohol that, to us, is undrinkable) which is liquid over a wider temperature range than is water.

The other basic ingredient of terrestrial life is carbon, which has the property of joining together with lots of other atoms to make the complex chemicals of life. Is there a substitute for carbon? The only real rival is silicon, which is a major constituent of rocks and is hence plentiful on planetary surfaces. Silicon is second only to carbon in its ability to link up into complex molecules, such as the silicon-oxygen chains known as silicones. Unfortunately, in nature silicon is most likely to bind with oxygen to form silicon dioxide (sand) and other rocky minerals known as silicates. Wherever we look in the Universe – in meteorites, comets, the atmospheres of the giant planets or interstellar clouds – all the interesting chemistry involves carbon, whereas silicon simply forms into rocks. Nature has clearly made its choice. Carbon is the preferred atom for complex chemistry, and its most likely ally for a solvent is water, if only because water is more abundant throughout the Galaxy than any alternative solvent. In short, there is nothing untoward about the biochemistry of life on Earth; car-

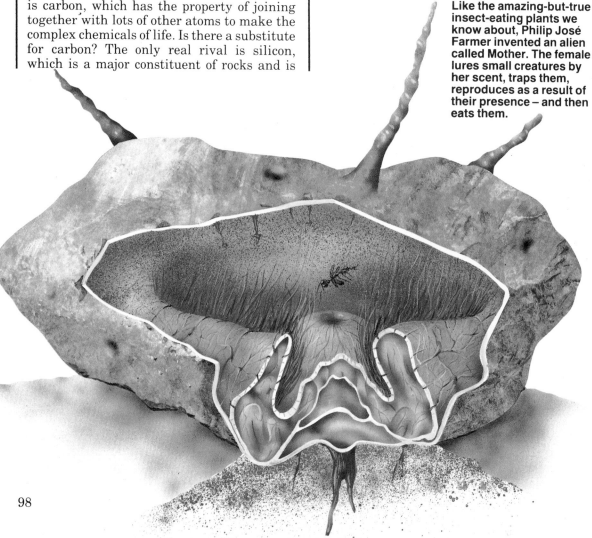

Like the amazing-but-true insect-eating plants we know about, Philip José Farmer invented an alien called Mother. The female lures small creatures by her scent, traps them, reproduces as a result of their presence – and then eats them.

98

bon and water are the best materials for the job, and so will they be on most other life-bearing planets.

But planets might not be the only sites for life. In the previous chapter we mentioned the idea by Fred Hoyle and Chandra Wickrama-singhe that living organisms might arise within comets shuttling through a cloud of gas in space. Could this be the first step towards the formation of some organized intelligent life in the clouds of space them-selves? Here the spectre of Hoyle's famous science fiction novel *The Black Cloud* raises its head. That fictional cloud had a size about equal to the diameter of the Earth's orbit and a mass two-thirds that of Jupiter. It had lived for 500 million years and was virtually immortal, moving from star to star where it recharged itself with energy. Its brain con-sisted of complex molecules on the surface of asteroid-like bodies that intercommunicated by radio, like a computer's memory banks. Gas flowing through the cloud served the same purpose as blood in a human. Perhaps somewhere out there – in the Orion nebula? – there is life between the stars.

Any large organism such as the Black Cloud is hampered in its speed of thinking and reaction by the time that a radio signal takes to pass across it, unless individual parts are programmed to deal with localized events. A similar drawback would befall the planet-wide intelligence Solaris, envisioned by Sta-nislaw Lem in his novel of the same name. Solaris is a water-covered planet slightly lar-ger than the Earth, and the organism is actually the ocean itself, which is capable of extruding a wide variety of features such as islands, domes, and even clouds.

In a way, the Earth itself behaves some-what like a planet-sized organism, which the English physicist James Lovelock has named Gaia, after the Greek goddess of Earth. Of course, it is not an intelligent organism; but Lovelock notes that the effect of all the living things on Earth has been to maintain condi-tions on our planet, such as temperature and atmospheric composition, so that they are suitable for the continued existence of life. This self-regulation of the Gaia organism has helped keep the Earth habitable despite the gradual increase in the Sun's luminosity over geological time.

Among the most bizarre speculations about life off Earth is the suggestion of life on a neutron star, the compressed core of matter left behind after the death of a large star. At first, the idea of life on such a body seems absurd: temperatures there would be above a million degrees, and the gravitational force would be a million million times that on Earth, so that a lofty mountain would be half a centimetre high. But look more closely, and you find that at the surface of a neutron star is a superdense sea of atomic particles, mostly protons and neutrons. These might link together by means of the so-called strong nuclear force which operates between atomic particles, thereby forming complex chains analogous to the molecules of terrestrial life. Under the exotic conditions on a neutron star, life would exist for a fleeting instant, perhaps a thousand million millionth of a second. But on the timescale of atomic particles, such a lifespan would be equivalent to months or years on Earth. Therefore, in the blinking of an eye whole generations of atomic particle organisms could live and die on a neutron star – or so the speculation runs.

Let us return from the realm of the fantastic to the more familiar ground of life based on carbon and water. Even here we find many ways in which the chemistry of life off Earth could differ from our own. For instance, the proteins in living organisms on Earth are made up from 20 different amino acids. But hundreds of other amino acids occur in nature, and there seems no particular reason why just those 20 should have been chosen for life on Earth. From all the possible amino acids, there are sufficient permutations to allow a unique set of amino acids for life on each planet in the Galaxy. Explorers visiting an alien planet would be well advised not to eat the local plants and animals – they could be indigestible, or positively poisonous.

How large can an alien be? That depends on many things, but there are certain guidelines. For instance, if you suddenly became twice as tall and broad as you are now, you would collapse because your weight would increase eight times, beyond the carrying power of

TYPE 1   **TYPE 2**   **TYPE 3**   **TYPE 4**

Three types of aliens have been 'identified' by an American UFO watchers' network, based on descriptions from many parts of the world. Type 1's are dwarfish creatures about a metre high, with a large head, penetrating if not glowing eyes and pale skins. Nobody has reported a 'little green man'. Type 2's are more like humans and, apart from the flesh creeping sensations they arouse, can be mistaken for them. Type 3's are hairy, two legged beings with glowing eyes. Type 4's change too much to be illustrated. Some are invisible.

human bones and muscles. Similar engineering problems apply to all large creatures, plus the problem of collecting sufficient food to satisfy a large bulk.

A planet's gravity, too, will affect the size and shape of aliens. On a high-gravity world, humanoid creatures would be shorter and stockier, whereas on a low-gravity world we might expect slim, gracefully shaped creatures with larger nostrils to breathe the thinner air. A low-gravity world might favour soaring trees and giraffe-like creatures to nibble at them, plus insects with prodigious leaping abilities. On a high-gravity world, particularly one with a dense atmosphere, octopus-like creatures or floating jelly fish might flourish.

Climate and environment would also affect the appearance of aliens. A being on a cold, snowy planet might be covered with white fur, like a polar bear. Were our Sun a hotter star, we might all be covered with reptile-like scales to protect against its radiation.

How many limbs would aliens be likely to

have? There are good arguments in favour of the efficiency of an arrangement of two arms and legs like our own, but some creatures on Earth have developed an odd number of limbs – the elephant, for instance, which uses its trunk as an extra arm, and the kangaroo and the extinct dinosaur *Tyrannosaurus rex*, in which the tail serves as a third leg. Monkeys also use their tails as extra limbs when manoeuvring in the trees. Starfish have odd numbers of limbs – usually five.

Extra eyes seem of less use than extra limbs, but they are possible. For instance, rattlesnakes have infra-red sensors for locating prey in addition to normal eyes. Some aliens might have a third, larger eye to detect heat radiated by living bodies. More than one mouth is possible, too – the functions of eating, breathing, and speaking need not all be accomplished through the same vent. Various other sensors are possible, such as for detecting the polarization of light from the sky or the planet's magnetic field, thus giving the creatures a homing ability rivalling that of pigeons or bees. Very large alien creatures could have more than one brain.

Aliens of every kind have been imagined by science fiction writers. Foremost among the tripeds is Larry Niven's remarkable Puppeteer. In addition to its three legs this creature has two heads, each on the end of a long neck. Each head has one eye, a mouth which functions like a hand, but no brain. The brain instead lies in a hump between the necks, and allows each head to talk independently. Writer Damon Knight invented the appealingly symmetrical Triped, a creature shaped rather like a pin in a bowling alley, with three legs, three arms, and a six-sided head with an eye in each side. A Triped breathes through the top of its head; in addition it has three slit-like mouths, one between each pair of arms. The Masters are another tripedal race, invented by writer John Christopher, conical in shape with three eyes arranged in a triangle, three tentacles, and two mouths, one for eating and the other for breathing and talking. The Masters move by rotating from one leg to another.

Six-legged creatures (hexapods) are plausible, particularly on worlds where land mammals have evolved from fish with three pairs of fins. Six legs give added stability and support on high-gravity planets. Coordinating several pairs of legs should be no problem – spiders and insects on Earth do it without difficulty. Some six-legged aliens could resemble centaurs, creatures in human mythology which had the torso of a man attached to the body and legs of a horse. A centaur-like alien would combine great mobility with manual dexterity.

But are legs necessary at all? Beings on a planet with extensive plains might evolve locomotion involving an organic version of ball bearings or roller castors. Piers Anthony, in his story *Cluster*, described creatures called Polarians from a hypothetical planet of the star Polaris. The Polarians are shaped like large tadpoles two metres long. At one end they have a large ball controlled by muscles on which they roll along at over 100 km/h.

Flight is an effective mode of transportation that has independently evolved in many forms of life on Earth – not just birds and insects but also reptiles (the Pterodactyl), mammals, and even fish. Gravity matters less than air pressure when it comes to flying. On a world with a dense atmosphere, birds could have the mass of a human, whereas in the thin air of Mars birds could hardly fly at all, despite the reduced gravity. The devil-like Overlords of Arthur C. Clark's novel *Childhood's End*, large entities with leathery wings, came from a low-gravity world with a dense atmosphere.

In *The Voyage of the Space Beagle*, A. E. van Vogt wrote of birdlike creatures called the Riim, which stand upright but have shrunken vestiges of wings on their shoulders. In addition they possess arms with long, delicate fingers. The Riim have beaklike mouths; their heads and arms sprout tufts of feathers. James Tiptree Jr. has imagined aerial creatures called Tyreeans possessing balloon-like bodies and wings. They live on a planet with high winds, feeding on plants and animals blowing past. The Tyreeans propel themselves around by sucking in air through intakes at the front and expelling it from jets at the rear. On worlds like Jupiter with no solid surface but a windy atmosphere, airborne organisms might flourish.

Extraterrestrials might differ from us in wearing their skeletons outside their body, like the carapace of a crab. Such external skeletons are popular among insects. In *Masters of the Maze*, Avram Davidson imagined six-limbed creatures called Chulpex, descended from insects. Chulpex, who live in underground caverns, stand upright on two legs, but have a two-tier torso with two pairs of arms, the uppermost pair being the larger and stronger. On their back is a shell-like covering which is repeatedly shed and regrown as the Chulpex develops; its average height is similar to that of a human. Chulpex females lay eggs.

Insect-like creatures could possess considerable dexterity, as in the Cinruss imagined by author James White. The Cinruss have fly-like wings and six fragile legs; the creatures evolved on a low-gravity world to near-human size. Their sucker-tipped hands enable them to carry out delicate surgical operations. Alien insects might not need great individual intelligence, but instead could succeed through a high degree of social organization, as in ant colonies on Earth.

How will humans on planet Earth evolve in the future? Will we, for instance, continue to become more intelligent? Not necessarily. The brain might reorganize itself internally to change our thinking patterns, but human

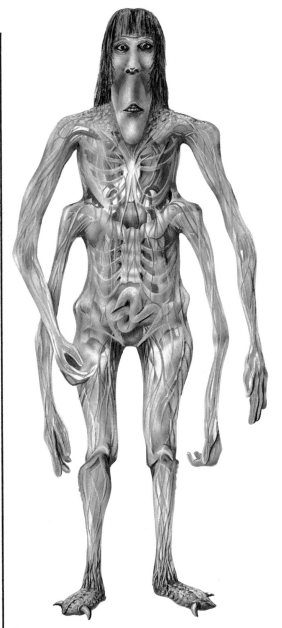

Descended from insects, the Chulpex creatures in Avram Davidson's Masters of the Maze, wear their skeletons outside their soft bodies as insects do.

brains can't become much larger than they are now because already they fill the human birth canal. In this respect, marsupial-like creatures would have the advantage, for the brains of their young could grow in the mother's pouch to a much larger size than is possible in the womb for human children. The pouch would have to act like an external womb to provide the carefully controlled environment that the human brain needs in which to develop.

Humans have one crucial difference from other life on Earth: they can change their environment to suit them, rather than having to change to fit the environment. For the first time, the Earth is inhabited by a species that can overcome the dictates of evolution. Medicine assists the survival of those individuals who would previously have died. Biological evolution, as it has acted on our ancestors in times past, may now be at an end. Our evolution from now on will be technological. Increases in brain size will no longer be necessary, for now we have computers to supplement human intelligence. Man-machine combinations, such as the Bionic Man of television fame, may be the new evolutionary step. Or perhaps intelligence is the very development that stifles evolutionary development, and so the race stagnates. Maybe that is why we see no extraterrestrials.

As a final 'what if', let us consider what would have happened on Earth if mankind had not arisen. Palaeontologists are agreed that it was the extinction of the dinosaurs 65 million years ago that allowed mammals to flourish in their place, starting a chain of development that eventually led to us. If the dinosaurs had not died out, it is likely that we, and the other large mammals, would not be here. But would there be something in our place? Dale Russell, a palaeontologist at the Museum of Natural Sciences in Ottawa, Canada, believes so. He has found fossil evidence that a small carnivorous dinosaur called Stenonychosaurus, about one metre tall, was developing a much larger brain than its dull-witted cousins. Had that development continued, Russell believes that by now the creature could have evolved into an upright-walking biped about 1.4 metres tall with a similar level of intelligence to our own.

In other words, had Stenonychosaurus and his kin not died out 65 million years ago, the creatures conquering space today from planet Earth would be intelligent lizards.

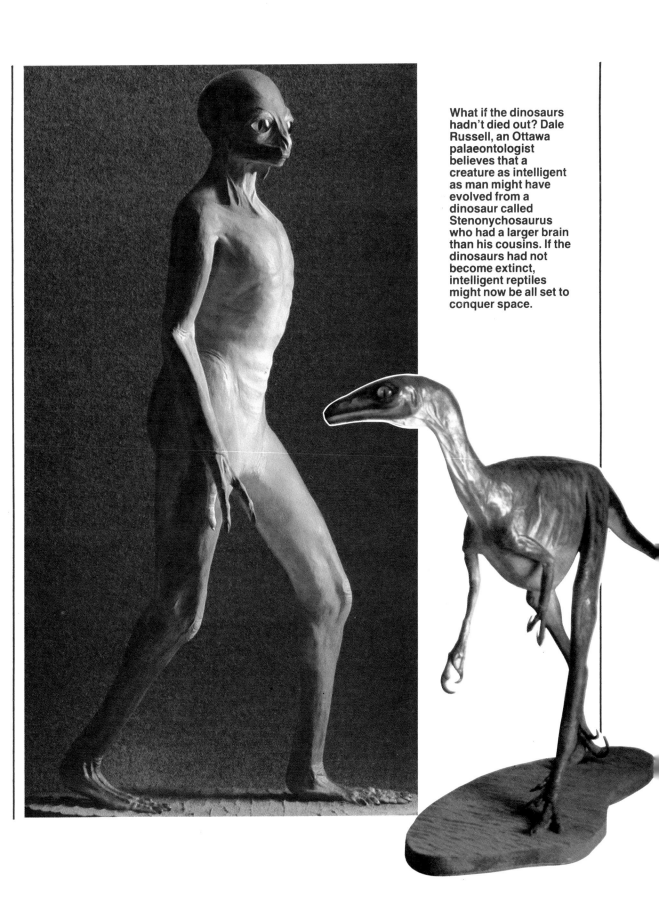

What if the dinosaurs hadn't died out? Dale Russell, an Ottawa palaeontologist believes that a creature as intelligent as man might have evolved from a dinosaur called Stenonychosaurus who had a larger brain than his cousins. If the dinosaurs had not become extinct, intelligent reptiles might now be all set to conquer space.

Chapter Nine

SEARCHING FOR OTHER BEINGS

On . . . off . . . on . . . off . . . a string of feeble radio pulses enters the metal ear of a dish-shaped radio telescope. Precisely timed, each pulse exactly the same length as the next, and all tuned to a single frequency – the hallmarks of an artificially generated transmission. In the control room next to the massive dish, radio astronomers play over their recording of the eerie signal. There can be no doubt. It is a message from other beings – the first proof that we are not alone in space.

That scene is still science fiction. But many astronomers believe that first contact with aliens will come in such a way, possibly before the end of the century.

For the humans of planet Earth, the era of interstellar communication arrived in 1960. In that year improvements in electronics and radio telescopes first made it possible for Earthbound astronomers to detect radio messages over interstellar distances. An American radio astronomer, Frank Drake, was eager to hear what cosmic chatter might be going on. In April 1960, he turned the 26-metre radio telescope of the National Radio Astronomy Observatory at Green Bank, West Virginia, towards two nearby stars. These stars, Tau Ceti and Epsilon Eridani, were chosen because of their similarity to the Sun, and their proximity to us, 12 and 11 light years away respectively.

There are good reasons for expecting that radio, rather than some other form of signalling, is the preferred method for interstellar communication. For one thing, radio is cheaper and simpler than rival methods – the energy required to generate radio messages is less than to send, say, an intense beam of light or X-rays from a laser. An artificial radio signal will stand out easily against the background of natural radio emission from space, whereas even the most intense laser beam will be scarcely noticeable next to the brilliant light of a parent star. And radio signals penetrate the gas and dust clouds of space that block visible light. So startalk, if it is going on, is most probably being done by radio rather than by flashes of light or bursts of X-rays.

Frank Drake's listening attempt was whimsically called Project Ozma, after the princess of the imaginary land of Oz – a place very far away, difficult to reach, and populated by exotic beings. The star Tau Ceti proved quiet, but when Drake and his colleagues turned the radio telescope on the second star, Epsilon Eridani, they were startled to hear a loud succession of rapid pulses like a machine gun. Eventually the signal was traced to interference from a secret radar transmitter on a military aircraft. It was a sobering demonstration of the false alarms that lie in wait for those in search of extraterrestrial signals. Despite two months of careful listening, Drake heard no whispers from far-away exotic beings around Tau Ceti or Epsilon Eridani. So was no one there – or were they calling us on a different line?

That raises one of the biggest worries concerning communication with life off Earth: how can we hope to dial the right number on the cosmic telephone if there are no directories? To receive an incoming call from aliens in space we must literally be on the same wavelength as the transmitting civilization. The problem is, there are so many wavelengths to choose from. The radio spectrum ranges from a wavelength of about one millimetre up to wavelengths of several hundred metres, used for domestic radio broadcasting. To attempt to pick up a signal from an unknown direction from among such a wide range of possible wavelengths is a daunting task, a veritable search for a needle in a cosmic haystack.

Fortunately, we can narrow the range of possible wavelengths. At wavelengths longer than about 30 centimetres, background noise from natural sources in the Galaxy becomes obtrusive. Wavelengths shorter than a centimetre or so are absorbed by our atmosphere, though this would not be a drawback for receivers and transmitters located in space. What we really need to find is a wavelength that would seem an obvious choice not only to us, but also to any aliens.

Such a wavelength was proposed in 1959 by two astronomers at Cornell University, Giuseppe Cocconi and Philip Morrison. They noted that the prime radio channel of the Galaxy is the 21 centimetre wavelength emitted by hydrogen gas, the most abundant substance in the Universe. By plotting the radio emission from hydrogen gas, radio astronomers on Earth have been able to trace the spiral shape of our Milky Way Galaxy. Radio astronomers anywhere in space would know about hydrogen's 21-centimetre emission and would have radio receivers tuned to it. Therefore, concluded Cocconi and Morrison, the 21 centimetre hydrogen line is the natural wavelength for interstellar communication.

This powerful realization that we could specify a unique channel for startalk sparked off the modern era of interest in the search for extraterrestrial intelligence (known in the fraternity as SETI). Frank Drake carried out his Ozma search at 21 centimetres, not so much because it was the wavelength recommended by Cocconi and Morrison but because it was the only wavelength which his receiver was tuned to. (Radio telescope receivers are pre-set to certain specific wavelengths allocated for radio astronomy use, and are not designed for dial-twiddling across a wide range of stations as domestic radio receivers are).

Drake abandoned Project Ozma after his negative results from Tau Ceti and Epsilon Eridani, but his attempt had alerted other astronomers to the possibility of stumbling across alien signals. Following Drake's lead, Soviet astronomers in 1968 listened to a dozen or so selected stars, and by 1970 they had established a network of small radio aerials across the Soviet Union covering the whole sky (or as much of it as is visible from the latitude of the receivers) in search of radio pulses from alien transmitters. Back at Green Bank, two large new radio dishes had sprouted up between the West Virginia hills, with receivers far more sensitive than those used for Project Ozma. Radio astronomer Gerrit Verschuur realized that it was now worth trying another search in the hope of hearing fainter signals that might previously have been missed. So in 1972 Verschuur turned the Green Bank 140-foot (43-metre) and 300-foot (91-metre) dishes towards ten stars, including Tau Ceti, Epsilon Eridani, and Barnard's star, in a project flippantly titled Ozpa. But he heard no alien call signs.

There have been several false alarms. In 1963 Soviet astronomers detected variations in a radio source catalogued as CTA-102 which they at first thought might be manifestations of some form of alien engineering activity. CTA-102 turned out to be a quasar, a distant and natural radio source in the Universe.

A bigger surprise awaited radio astronomers at Cambridge, England, in 1967 when they picked up regular pulses coming from deep space at just over one-second intervals. Pulses so frequent and so precise seemed

Disappointed to find that they had not picked up a 'little green man', scientists at Cambridge in 1967 should at least have been pleased to pick up a pulsar for the first time.

suspiciously artificial. For a few weeks, the Cambridge team seriously considered the possibility that they had picked up a signal from another civilization. Only partly in jest they termed the source LGM, for Little Green Man. But the source was, it transpired, the first of the pulsars, tiny and highly condensed stars that flash like a lighthouse as they rapidly spin. More than 300 pulsars are now known.

The Russians were caught out for a second time when their transcontinental network registered 1½-second-long bleeps from a source in space. These pulses turned out to come from an Earth satellite, another example of the many sources of interference which exist to trap the unwary. The radio spectrum is now so crowded that man-made interference, even at the wavelengths preserved for radio astronomy, is the main problem for those in search of faint signals from life off Earth.

As of 1982, over 30 searches for extraterrestrial signals had been undertaken or were underway, mostly of very limited scope. Among the most ambitious searches was Ozma II undertaken at Green Bank, the spiritual home of SETI, by Benjamin Zuckerman and Patrick Palmer. From 1972 to 1976 they scanned over 650 of the nearest Sun-like stars

at 21 centimetre wavelength using the 300-foot (91-metre) and 140-foot (43-metre) dishes. No alien signals were picked up.

At Ohio State University, Robert Dixon and his colleagues began a continuous all-sky survey in 1973 using a wire-fence-like radio telescope that scans wide slabs of the sky as the Earth rotates. Surveying a wide area of sky rather than specific targets involves a sacrifice of sensitivity, but the advantage is that every star (and the space between them) is systematically covered. Connected to the telescope's receiver is a computer that prints out columns of figures from 1 to 9 on a paper strip; the higher the figure, the stronger the signal. On August 15, 1977 the telescope's beam passed across a source in the direction of the constellation Sagittarius of such strength that the computer began to print out letters of the alphabet, representing signal strengths up to 30 times greater than the background noise. An excited observatory worker circled that part of the printout in red ink and wrote 'Wow!' in the margin.

Two things were clear: the signal was artificial, because it was confined to a narrow range of frequencies, and it came from well beyond the Earth because it passed across the telescope's field of view as the Earth rotated. But despite weeks of rechecking the area of sky from which the signal came, it was never heard again.

Investigations by the Ohio astronomers failed to trace any space probes that could have caused the signal. Neither were there any Sun-like stars in the telescope's view that could have been the source. So the origin of the 'Wow!' signal remains a mystery. Probably it was interference from some unknown man-made source such as a distant satellite. But, say Dixon and his colleagues, it remains the nearest thing they have heard to an incoming call on the cosmic telephone.

To confound the SETI scene further, a wide range of alternative wavelengths has emerged to challenge the 21-centimetre hydrogen line as the most plausible channel for startalk. One leading rival is the wavelength around 18 centimetres emitted by a substance found commonly in space called hydroxyl, consisting of one hydrogen atom linked to one oxygen atom. SETI researchers have sifted the records of some radio telescopes, which tune in regularly to the hydroxyl wavelength, for signs of alien beacons.

Hydroxyl emissions were first detected from gas in space in 1963. Had Cocconi and Morrison written their paper at that time, they might have noted that the 18 centimetre hydroxyl line and the 21-centimetre hydrogen line stand like gateposts either side of the region of the radio spectrum in which background noise from space is quietest. Hydroxyl (chemical symbol OH) combines with hydrogen (symbol H) to make water (H_2O), so this region of the spectrum has become known as the water hole. Because of the importance of water to life as we know it, proponents of the water hole claim that it is the most obvious trunk route for cosmic phone calls. But to search the entire water hole is going to require considerably more effort than astronomers have expended on SETI so far.

Water molecules themselves exist in space. They emit radiation not in the region of the water hole, but at an entirely separate wavelength of 1.35 centimetres. Two Canadian astronomers, Paul Feldman and Alan Bridle, argue that this is also a plausible hailing frequency between extraterrestrials, and they have launched a listening project at 1.35 centimetres with the 150-foot (46-metre) radio telescope at Algonquin Park, Ontario.

In truth, there now seems little justification for favouring any particular wavelength for SETI. To be certain that we are not missing any signals in the cosmic haystack, we must be prepared to search the entire range of radio wavelengths that reach us on Earth. In recognition of this, scientists from NASA's Ames Research Center and Jet Propulsion Laboratory, both in California, have formulated plans for the most comprehensive SETI project yet undertaken. They will use existing radio telescopes for their search, but with a key new piece of equipment: a receiver capable of gulping in large swaths of the radio spectrum at a time and chopping it into narrow strips for analysis.

SETI researchers are agreed that incoming signals will be finely tuned to a precise frequency no wider than a few hertz (cycles per second), and possibly as narrow as one hundredth of a hertz. The reason is that, for a transmitter of given power, the signal will carry further, if the transmitter's power is squeezed into a narrow bandwidth. Against this is the drawback that ultra-narrow signals are more difficult to spot. Most of the SETI efforts to date used receivers with insufficient definition to pick out narrow-band signals; any faint bleeps would simply have been lost in the background hiss. Therefore there is every reason to start again with purpose-built equipment.

NASA plans to search in two complementary ways. One branch of the search will comb the whole sky at wavelengths between 3 centimetres and 25 centimetres, listening to frequency bands 32 hertz wide. While that is going on, other searchers will focus on more than 700 of the nearest stars like the Sun, listening from 10 centimetres to 25 centimetres for signals as narrow as 1 hertz. Particular emphasis will be placed on stars within 20 light years of the Earth in the expectation that, if the Galaxy has been widely colonized as some scientists believe, then signals are more likely to be coming to us from near at hand rather than from far away.

The device that makes the whole project feasible is a sophisticated piece of electronics called a multi-channel spectrum analyser (MCSA) which listens to nearly 8 million possible incoming call channels simultaneously. After turning its ear to all these channels for a few minutes, the MCSA moves on to the next part of the radio spectrum, and so on. A computer checks any incoming signals to ensure they are not simply due to man-made interference or are from some known astronomical source before it alerts project scientists. However, NASA's SETI people are resigned to winnowing their way through endless chaff before finding a genuine alien signal – if any exists, that is.

NASA's plans received official approval at the end of 1982 when the U.S. Congress authorized a budget of $1½ million a year for SETI. The project got under way in mid 1983 with the testing at the Goldstone deep-space tracking station of a 74,000-channel receiver, a prototype of the eventual 8-million channel receiver.

Meanwhile, an independent SETI programme had been begun in March 1983 by Professor Paul Horowitz of Harvard University, utilizing the 84-foot (26-metre) radio dish at Harvard's Agassiz station in Massachusetts. Plugged in to this radio telescope is a 128,000-channel receiver built by Horowitz with a grant from the privately funded Planetary Society. Every six months the antenna sweeps the sky from 60° north to 30° south while the receiver listens for signals a mere 0.015 hertz wide around a certain preselected wavelength such as the 21 centimetre hydrogen line or the 18 centimetre hydroxyl line. Once the sky has been scanned at one wavelength, Horowitz switches to another wavelength and repeats the search. Although immensely sensitive, the Horowitz search is limited in the number of wavelengths it can cover, which the full-scale NASA search will not be. So widespread is the enthusiasm for SETI that a number of American radio amateurs, guided by NASA scientists, are now setting up their own private listening stations for incoming alien signals – a kind of CB SETI.

NASA's scientists will use the 210-foot (64-metre) space-probe tracking antennas of the Deep Space Network at Goldstone in California, Madrid in Spain and Tidbinbilla in Australia, plus the 1,000-foot (305-metre) dish at Arecibo in Puerto Rico. NASA's SETI team estimates that their whole project will take ten years – five years to develop the advanced electronics, and another five years for the search itself. The total outlay will be about the same as the budget for a movie such as E.T. By the end of the project they will have picked their way through 10 million times more of the cosmic haystack than all previous SETI efforts put together. That should be enough to tell us whether or not anyone is trying to attract our attention. By

In November 1974, the huge dish telescope at Arecibo in Puerto Rico beamed out a message towards the M13 cluster of stars in the constellation Hercules. We cannot expect a reply before AD 52000!

1993, therefore, we could have picked up our first interstellar call.

Assuming that somebody really does ring NASA's bell, what might we expect to hear from the aliens? Their message might be similar to one sent out from the world's largest radio telescope, 305 metres in diameter, operated by Cornell University and nestled among the mountains at Arecibo in Puerto Rico. For three minutes in November 1974, that mighty dish pumped out the most powerful radio signal ever sent by mankind: a stream of 1,679 staccato pulses of energy. The significance of the figure 1,679 is that it is the product of two prime numbers, 23 and 73. By arranging pulses into a grid 23 characters wide by 73 deep, the alien recipients will reconstruct a dot picture like a mosaic telling them something about life on Earth (see illustration).

Pictograms such as this are an attractive way of conveying a lot of information in a simple fashion, but our cosmic cousins may prefer more sophisticated signals involving mathematics or some kind of language best interpreted by a computer. The Arecibo message was beamed towards a cluster of 300,000 stars known to astronomers as M 13 in the constellation Hercules. Even if there is anyone there to receive it, the cluster is so far away that the message, travelling at the speed of light, will take 25,000 years to get there. The earliest we could expect a reply is around AD 52,000.

A three-minute signal transmitted to such a distant target is hardly a serious attempt at announcing our presence to life off Earth. But the Arecibo message has already been studied by countless recipients – here on Earth. Its true significance is to awaken mankind to the fact that, if intelligent life does exist off Earth, contact with it is inevitable. So we had better be prepared.

What if the aliens are not deliberately trying to attract our attention? Listening carefully with our largest radio telescopes, we could eavesdrop on their domestic transmissions leaking through their planet's ionosphere into space. And, conversely, anyone out there could already be tuned to ABC, BBC,

DIALLING THE COSMOS

This is our message to the star cluster M13 (far right): a string of on-off radio pulses, represented by noughts and ones, which can be arranged into a picture telling aliens about life on Earth without the need to know a word of our language.

Aliens should quickly recognize that the top line of the message contains the numbers one to ten written from right to left in the binary code used by computers. Below that is a block of five numbers – 1, 6, 7, 8, and 15 – which chemists will recognize as the atomic number of the main ingredients of life, hydrogen, carbon, nitrogen, oxygen, and phosphorus. Then come the chemical formulae of the component parts of the genetic material DNA. Molecules of DNA form themselves into a double spiral staircase structure. This information about biochemistry of life off Earth leads to the robot-like figure of a human, bracketed by numbers which show his height and the population of Earth.

Under his feet is a simple map of the solar system with the third planet from the Sun offset to show its connection with the human figure. At the bottom, the Arecibo telescope is depicted beaming the signal into space. All this is contained in a three-minute broadcast consisting of 1,679 pulses of radio energy – an indication of how much information could easily be transferred from star to star.

CBS, NBC, and the other major TV and radio stations around the globe.

Some scientists such as Britain's Astronomer Royal, radio astronomer Sir Martin Ryle, have urged that we should keep radio silence for fear of attracting the attention of potentially hostile extraterrestrials. But already it is too late. Extraterrestrials of similar technological level to ourselves could detect TV broadcasts from Earth at a distance of 25 light years, a range encompassing about 300 stars, and would receive beams from our ballistic missile early warning radars at 250 light years or more, a range encompassing several hundred thousand stars. According to astronomer Woodruff Sullivan and his colleagues at the University of Washington, Seattle, eavesdropping aliens could by now have put together a detailed picture of life on our planet, including an assessment of our defence capabilities.

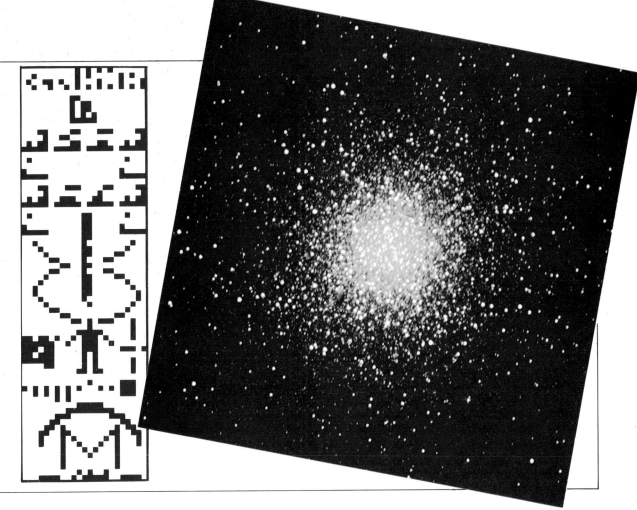

Most of the radio noise leaking into space comes from the 2,000 or so most powerful TV and radio transmitters in North America and western Europe. Even more intense are the transmissions from missile-watching early warning radars. An alien civilization with large radio telescopes might have its attention drawn first by these intense radar beams, but it would in the long run be able to extract most information about life on Earth from our domestic TV broadcasts.

Inhabitants of Alpha Centauri and points beyond will not be glued to their screens for each weekly episode of *Star Trek*, because programme information itself will be too weak to decipher over interstellar distances. But the aliens will be able to receive the powerful carrier waves on which the programmes ride.

By careful analysis of the slight frequency changes of the signals during a year, caused by the Doppler shift as the Earth moves around the Sun, the aliens would be able to deduce the size of the Earth's orbit and hence, knowing our distance from the Sun, to predict the likely temperature of our planet. Knowing that we are in the liquid-water zone around our parent star, the aliens could deduce that we are air-breathing, water-drinking beings. By observing the rising and setting of various transmitting stations as the Earth rotates, the aliens would be able to measure the length of our day, and the diameter and axial tilt of the Earth.

An estimate of the size of TV transmitting antennae would also be possible, thereby giving some indication of the scale of engineering structures on Earth. This, allied to knowledge of our planet's size, would enable the aliens to estimate the strength of our gravity and the likely size of a human.

A really inquisitive extraterrestrial who

listened in turn to each of the 2,000 or so most powerful TV transmitters on Earth could plot their positions to within a few miles, thus drawing a rough map of Earth. Different broadcast schedules of various transmitters, combined with the locations of the various early warning radars operated by the two superpowers, could reveal the political divisions of our planet. That much an alien could learn without even visiting us.

The Arecibo message is not the only deliberate calling card from Earth travelling to the stars. In 1972 and 1973 two space probes, Pioneer 10 and Pioneer 11, set course for the outer planets. Their outward flight, having taken them past their targets Jupiter and Saturn, is now leading them irreversibly away from the Sun and towards the stars. They will not pass close to any nearby stars, but in case some civilization should intercept them as their meteorite-battered hulks drift silently through the Galaxy in millions of years to come, each Pioneer carries a 23 by 15-centimetre gold-plated aluminium plaque etched with an intriguing pictorial greeting from Earth (or, more precisely, from Carl Sagan and Frank Drake).

At top left of the plaque is a representation of the hydrogen atom, which broadcasts the familiar 21-centimetre wavelength radiation. At the bottom is a sketch of our solar system, showing the path of Pioneer 10 past Jupiter (Pioneer 11 was subsequently rerouted to pass Saturn as well, but both probes carry the same plaque). Left centre of the plaque is a spider-like pattern representing the position of 14 pulsars relative to the Sun. This information will allow aliens to work out the approximate position of our star. Along each of the lines pointing to a pulsar is a series of tick marks indicating the pulsar's frequency of pulsation. The pulsation rate of pulsars slows down with age, so aliens will be able to estimate when the probe was launched by comparing the observed rate of each pulsar when the probe is found with the rate indicated on the plaque.

Finally, drawn against an outline of the Pioneer spacecraft itself are two human figures, male and female. The male has his right hand raised in what is intended to be a greeting of friendship – though it might not be interpreted that way in another part of the Galaxy!

Following in the tracks of Pioneer 10 and 11 are the two Voyager probes, each of which will also end up lost among the stars and each of which carries a far richer message than the Pioneer plaques: a long-playing record, into the grooves of which are encoded colour pictures, spoken greetings, Earth sounds, and a selection of music. The 30-centimetre gold-plated copper discs come in an aluminium cover engraved with instructions for playing them at $16\frac{2}{3}$ rpm. A stylus and cartridge accompany each record.

And if the aliens do play the record, what will they find? For the first ten minutes or so they will hear noise; not any random noise, but actually picture information converted into sound. By converting the audio signals back into electronic signals, the aliens can construct 116 pictures, in colour and black and white, depicting various aspects of the Earth and life upon it. First comes a tour of the solar system, then details about human cells, anatomy, and reproduction. A photograph of a naked pregnant woman was censored by NASA – some American citizens had objected to the nude figures on the Pioneer plaque as 'filth'. Instead of the photograph, a silhouette drawing was substituted, doubtless to the confusion of any alien recipient.

Landscapes of the Earth follow, showing plants, animals, and examples of various human races and culture from across the globe. Famous buildings, including the Taj Mahal, Sydney Opera house, and the United Nations headquarters are illustrated. The picture sequence ends with examples of high technology – roads, a railway, a bridge, aero-

Now voyaging beyond the Solar System, Pioneer 10 carries a message from mankind; a series of scientific symbols from which it could be calculated who sent the craft and where it came from. The hydrogen atom is used as a 'clock' and 'yardstick' giving the time of Pioneer's departure and the size of the creatures who sent it. Across the bottom are the planets with the spacecraft's trajectory clearly indicated. Let us hope that the man's hand raised in a gesture of goodwill is looked at first by a creature of equally benign intention.

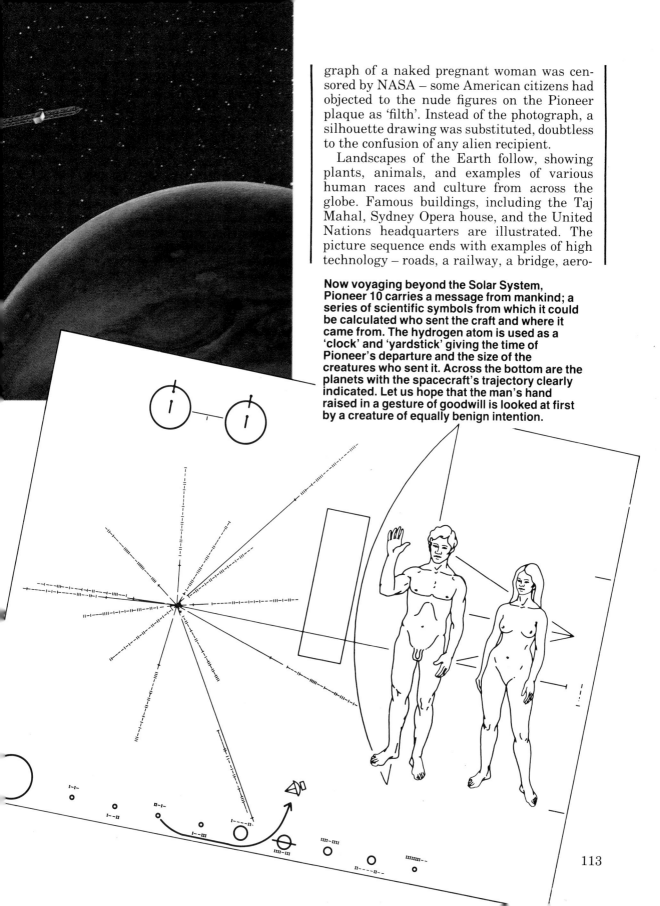

planes, a radio telescope, and a rocket.

Then come spoken greetings in 55 different languages, representing nearly 90 per cent of the people on Earth. Extraterrestrial linguists will have fun listening to such varied wishes as 'Good health to you now and forever,' in Welsh, 'Let there be peace everywhere,' in Bengali, 'Hello to the residents of far skies,' in Persian, and the slightly worrisome invitation in Amoy: 'Have you eaten yet? Come visit us if you have time.'

Next, the alien listeners will hear a 12-minute essay in sound intended to portray our planet and its teeming life. The first sounds signify the primeval stirrings of the planet – volcanoes, earthquakes, wind, rain, thunder, and surf – in the billions of years before life itself began to add its voice to the sounds of Earth. We hear a variety of animals, and then the sound of footsteps signifies the emergence of upright walking primates. Human speech makes an appearance, followed by the sounds of civilization including the herding of sheep, a blacksmith's shop, and a farmer's tractor. The development of transport is illustrated by sounds ranging from ships, a horse and cart, trains, and road vehicles, to an aircraft and the launch of a Saturn V. Rounding out the sound essay are the sounds of a kiss, a mother and child, someone's brain-wave pattern (will any extraterrestrial ever interpret those thoughts?), and the steady ticking of a pulsar.

The last 87½ minutes of the total two-hour recording consists of 27 selections of music, irreverently known as Earth's Greatest Hits. As with other parts of the message, it represents a wide range of cultures and times. Bach is represented by three compositions and Beethoven by two, among them the first movement of the Fifth Symphony, at over 7 minutes the longest piece of music on the record. The shortest piece is a wedding song from Peru, just over half a minute long. Other selections include a Navajo Indian ceremonial night chant, the harmonious sounds of Melanesian panpipes, the birdlike cry of a Japanese bamboo flute solo, the drone of an Australian aboriginal didgeridoo, Louis Armstrong's Melancholy Blues, and Johnny B. Goode by Chuck Berry. Long after most of the artefacts of our civilization have vanished, the Pioneer and Voyager probes will drift among the stars bearing their cosmic messages in a bottle, time capsules from 20th century Earth.

Space probes can be loaded with considerably more information than a simple engraved plaque or a long-playing record. Whole libraries of information could be stored in the computer brain of an interstellar probe, such as the self-reproducing probes discussed in Chapter 6. Some astronomers have argued that messenger probes, rather than radio signals, are the best way for an advanced civilization to contact another. Such a probe could heave to around a likely star and wait until it detected the first signs of an emergent civilization's radio traffic. Then, at an opportune moment, it could beam selected excerpts from its stored program to the planet and invite an interchange of messages without the many centuries of waiting that would be inevitable when trading messages between stars hundreds of light years apart. If nothing else, as mathematician Frank Tipler of Tulane University, New Orleans, has pointed out, a messenger probe could construct a massive sign saying 'Drink Coca Cola' and put it in orbit around the inhabited planet.

In addition to searching for possible incoming calls on the cosmic telephone, we should also search our own solar system for signs of alien explorer probes or even space colonies populated by alien beings. Perhaps some of the objects we have hitherto taken to be asteroids are actually alien vehicles, mingling with natural asteroids in the richest source of readily available raw materials in our solar system.

And there are some strangely shaped asteroids: Eros, for instance, is highly elongated, and Hektor seems to be double, or at least peanut-shaped. Numerous asteroids are suspected to be accompanied by smaller satellites rather like escort ships around the flagship of a fleet. There is no suggestion that these are anything other than natural bodies, but some of the smaller, unregarded asteroids should be examined for evidence of artificiality. The irony is that, while we have been concentrating on examining far-off stars, the aliens may have been on our doorstep all the time.

Chapter Ten

UFOs

If life really does exist out there, and if interstellar travel is possible, is someone already doing it? Could there be alien versions of Captain Kirk and the starship Enterprise roaming the Galaxy, and perhaps even be arriving here to discover us? Advanced civilizations, if they exist, could already have colonized the Galaxy, as we saw in Chapter 8. Perhaps there is an alien base in the solar system keeping an eye on us.

Imagine the sensation that news of Earthmen would cause to a distant civilization. On a small, blue-green planet orbiting an unassuming yellow-white star, an ape-descended lifeform is entering the age of space exploration and interstellar communication. Its population is swelling to unprecedented proportions, while its energy reserves dwindle to critical levels. Will this fledgling civilization survive? Should contact be made and assistance provided?

According to one widely publicized view, alien starships are indeed surveying the Earth, possibly in preparation for a full-scale landing. Increasingly persistent stories claim that contact has already been made, at least in a limited way, and that humans have met aliens. Such first-hand evidence of life off Earth would be of staggering significance, as sensational to us as were, in their day, the tales of ancient mariners who had visited far off lands and traded with the natives. Yet scientists, on the whole, have not taken the stories of alien spacefarers seriously.

News of alleged alien visits is confined to popular newspapers, where it jostles for attention with the private lives of film stars, astrological predictions, claims of spoons bent by psychic forces, haunted houses, and other escapist fodder. Have humans been too eager to embrace a romantic myth, or are scientists too narrow-minded to perceive the signs in the sky?

Those 'signs', of course, are popularly termed unidentified flying objects, or UFOs. Now that the subject is so fashionable, it is not difficult to find someone who has seen a UFO. My own experience in debates on this subject is that up to half the population are willing to subscribe to the proposition that UFOs are extraterrestrial spacecraft. This is a staggeringly high level of belief.

Of course, not all reported UFOs can be extraterrestrial spacecraft, and no one pretends they are. For a start, nine out of every ten UFO reports is readily explained in known terms and hence becomes an IFO. The rest remain unidentified – which means they could be anything. It may seem strange that a sighting which remains unidentified should actually be used as evidence for extraterrestrial visitation, but that is a measure of the assumptions inherent in the field. Unfortunately, despite 35 years of searching, there are no Identified Alien Spaceships.

A cornerstone of the UFO believers' case is that UFOs are reported by trained observers and other highly credible persons whose eye witness testimony would readily be accepted in a court of law. For instance, UFOlogists were delighted in 1976 when Jimmy Carter, then a candidate for the United States presidency, reported that seven years earlier he and ten other witnesses had watched a brilliant UFO low on the horizon which appeared to move towards them and away again, apparently changing in brightness, size, and

colour. Carter estimated that the UFO was between 300 yards and 1,000 yards from him, and said that at times it became as big and bright as the full Moon. By any standards, Carter must be regarded as a highly credible witness, for in addition to his political standing he is a former naval officer trained in celestial navigation and a Naval Academy graduate in nuclear physics.

But, as is invariably the case in UFO matters, things were not as good as they seemed. When American UFO researcher Robert Sheaffer investigated the sighting, he had great trouble finding any of Carter's companions that night who remembered the incident. Eventually he found one who vaguely recalled looking at a light he thought might have been a balloon. That is hardly the vivid sight described by Carter.

What is more, it emerged that Carter was nine months out in his recollection of the date. Once the correct date had been established, astronomical records showed that the planet Venus had been at its most brilliant in the sky exactly where Carter had reported his UFO. And Venus is by far the most common cause of UFO reports. UFOlogists have argued that Carter was a reliable observer who would not be likely to mistake Venus for a UFO. However, it seems odd that he did not describe the UFO's position relative to Venus – above, below, or whatever. In fact, he did not even mention Venus, even though it was the most conspicuous object in that part of the sky. There seems no reasonable doubt that Carter's UFO was actually Venus.

Note that Sheaffer's investigation revealed many errors in the original report: the size and brightness of the object is overestimated, the distance is underestimated, and spurious motion is attributed to the object. But such errors are typical of those made by people observing bright celestial objects. Carter is in good company in misidentifying Venus. Sheaffer investigated a hilarious 100 mph police chase of Venus through Ohio and Pennsylvania in 1966. They never caught it, but they did inspire a scene in the movie *Close Encounters of the Third Kind.*

Aircraft pilots are another class of UFO reporters whom UFOlogists rate highly. An impressive case occurred in 1969 when pilots aboard a commercial jet flying at a height of 12 kilometres over the United States described a formation of four objects emitting a blue-green flame which buzzed the airliner at an estimated distance of 100 metres. This was in daylight, not at night. A military jet flying some miles behind the airliner reported a squadron of UFOs heading towards him that suddenly seemed to climb as if under intelligent control.

At the same time as this UFO encounter a brilliant daylight fireball (a piece of natural debris from space burning up high in the atmosphere) broke up into several flaming pieces over the United States. Brilliant daylight fireballs are very rare, and there seems little doubt that this object was what the pilots saw. Despite their impression of a near-collision with a squadron of metallic craft under intelligent control, the fireball was at least 150 kilometres from them. So even experienced pilots can make major errors of identification and distance. That does not make them bad airmen, simply human.

Animal effects are often taken as confirming the reality of UFO sightings. In 1968 a woman science teacher in Ohio reported three saucer-shaped UFOs flying in military formation. She had a PhD and served in the Navy during World War II – the sort of witness you would consider highly reliable and not given to fantasy. She flashed a torch at the saucers, but they did not flash back. She reported that during the incident her dog lay down and whimpered.

Unknown to her she was actually seeing the Russian Zond 4 spacecraft burning up in the atmosphere. It turned out that the dog whimpered because it hated the cold, and the temperature on the night that its owner dallied to flash messages at a passing UFO was eight degrees below freezing. Humans can make mistakes about animal behaviour as well as about UFOs.

A close encounter with a flying saucer is a familiar theme in UFO books. But the vast majority of UFO sightings are misidentifications of natural or man-made objects, fuelled by the imagination of witnesses who now expect to see alien craft

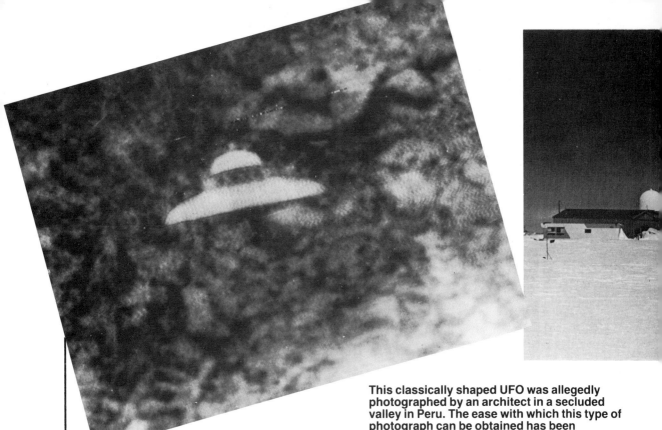

This classically shaped UFO was allegedly photographed by an architect in a secluded valley in Peru. The ease with which this type of photograph can be obtained has been repeatedly demonstrated.

No one denies that UFOs exist in the sense that people see things that they cannot identify. But the important question is: what do these things turn out to be on investigation? Let me quote the experience of one of the world's most active UFO investigators, Allan Hendry of the Center for UFO Studies in Illinois, which operates a telephone hotline for receiving UFO reports. Hendry has published the results of his investigations in a book called The UFO Handbook (required reading for anyone seriously interested in the subject). Of 1,300 cases that he investigated, he was able to identify 91 per cent. His results confirm other studies in showing that the main offenders are bright stars and planets, aircraft, meteors, and satellites – although a complete list of misidentifications would be almost endless.

We really want to know about the nine per cent residue that remained unexplained. UFOlogists always take the unexplained residue to show that there must be something to UFOs after all. But that's not so. Hendry does not think that the remaining UFOs are anything different from the identifieds – he just could not pin down the correct mundane explanation in each case. In other words, while we must always allow for the existence of something unknown to explain UFO reports, there is no compelling evidence for it. Equally you do not need to invent a whole race of alien criminals to account for unsolved crimes. The fact that a report may be unexplained is not evidence of any theory.

Some of the cases that Hendry solved sound on a first hearing to have no conceivable terrestrial explanation. There was a 1978 UFO near Chicago which witnesses sketched as a saucer with a dome on top and rotating lights around its exterior. According to the scared witnesses it was as large as a football field, it followed a car at treetop level, it hovered, caused a TV set to black out, and finally departed in the blink of an eye.

The actual cause was an advertising plane – a light aircraft carrying electric bulbs which flash out advertising messages. (Someone else who once reported an advertising

Reflection of light in the camera lens accounts for this glowing saucer that turned up on a picture by a scientist from an Arctic weather station. Such reflections are a common cause of UFOs on film.

George Adamski claimed that this photograph showed a Venusian scout ship, but multiple reflections make it look like a small model under artificial lighting.

plane as a UFO said: 'I had the strange feeling that it was trying to say something.')

In an even more astounding case, three witnesses reported a saucer 7.6 metres in diameter accompanied by two pulsating lights which hovered over a hospital car park for nearly an hour, dimming the car park lights as though sucking power from them. A humming noise was heard which changed to a loud beeping before the saucer shot straight up into the sky. A parakeet owned by one of the witnesses screeched and her dogs barked. The woman felt as though she were in a trance and could hardly speak or move. This has all the hallmarks of a classic UFO case: electromagnetic effects, animal reactions, and physical effects on the witness.

However, Hendry determined that the witnesses were looking at the crescent Moon (the 'saucer') with Mars and Jupiter next to it (the 'pulsating lights'). The dimming of the lights in the car park was caused by intermittent mist which eventually obscured the Moon and planets. The rest of the report is a marvellous product of human imagination.

It is only a small step from imagining a flying saucer to imagining its occupants. Hendry investigated a close encounter of the third kind, as these occupant sightings are called, stimulated by Venus. A woman reported that a very bright object in the southwest had made a slow, jerky descent over a period of an hour one evening. She became convinced as she stared at it that she could see occupants with rounded, silvery heads staring out of windows on the UFO. The UFO turned up again on subsequent nights, exactly where Venus should be. Faced with cases like these, one wonders how far it is possible to credit any UFO report.

The limitations of human eyewitness testimony have been further demonstrated by a British UFO researcher, David Simpson, in a series of controlled hoaxes on groups of UFO spotters who were congregated for communal sky watches. Simpson suspended a 3-volt torch bulb beneath a kite or balloon and flew it in the vicinity of the unsuspecting UFO watchers. Their responses were truly remarkable: 'It was brighter than any man-made light'; 'It was definitely metallic and had portholes'; 'It out-manoeuvred any known aircraft'; 'I flashed my torch and it flashed the same code back'; 'It communicated with me telepathically'.

A more elaborate hoax was perpetrated on a group of UFO spotters observing from Cradle Hill at Warminster, Wiltshire, the spiritual home of the British UFO movement. From a neighbouring hill, Simpson shone a bright purple light towards the startled UFO watchers. Among them was an accomplice of his, who pretended to photograph the light. He then gave the roll of negatives to one of the UFOlogists for processing and study.

Unknown to the UFOlogist, however, the film had already been exposed to show a different part of the horizon with a flying saucer superimposed. When processed, the film was found to contain four exposed frames, on two of which the fake flying saucer appeared. This fake flying saucer looked nothing like the simple light which had actually appeared that night; it was on a different part of the horizon from the real light; it had moved between frames, whereas the purple light had been stationary; and there were other inconsistencies which showed that all four frames could not have been taken at the same time from the same place.

Despite all these deliberate clues, UFOlogists never spotted the hoax. From 1970 to 1971, *Flying Saucer Review*, the world's leading UFO magazine, published ten articles about the Warminster photographs. The magazine's photographic consultant pronounced the negatives genuine. They were also endorsed by a noted French astronomer, Dr Pierre Guerin. If such an obvious hoax is so readily accepted by UFOlogists, it is hardly surprising that the annals of UFOlogy are riddled with unreliable cases.

Photographs of UFOs are, unfortunately, all too easy to fake. Those that are not fakes turn out to be natural or man-made objects such as clouds, stars, birds, and planes, or faults such as lens flare, reflections from windows, and processing defects. Cine film of UFOs is much more difficult to fake, and much rarer. Therefore I was intrigued to learn in 1978 of three minutes of film showing glowing UFOs taken near Stonehenge in Wiltshire by a family on holiday. According to the eyewitnesses, the objects had appeared as though out of thin air, manoeuvred, gathered into a V-shaped formation, and disappeared in a manner that seemed to defy any conventional explanation. The cine film had been examined and declared genuine by Kodak photo analysts. On the face of it, this film promised to become one of the most significant pieces of UFO evidence. Some expert opinions were needed.

Accordingly, I arranged a viewing session of the film for a scientific audience at Kodak's London offices, in conjunction with UFO researchers Jenny Randles and Peter Warrington who were investigating the film. Working on the assumption that the film might show some rare atmospheric electrical phenomenon akin to ball lightning, I invited to the viewing several physicists with an interest in atmospheric phenomena, plus an army munitions expert. It soon emerged that the objects had nothing to do with ball lightning, nor with alien spaceships. If the eyewitness descriptions were ignored and the film viewed impartially, the objects could be readily explained as nothing more exotic than military flares suspended under parachutes – not a surprising conclusion since the Salisbury Plain area around Stonehenge is a military range, which is why I had taken the precaution of asking along a munitions expert. My sobering experience with this film finally convinced me that eyewitness reports can never be taken at face value. Unfortunately, eyewitness reports are usually all we have to go on, which is why so many sightings remain unexplained. Without the objective evidence of the film, this Stonehenge case would have remained unexplained.

What about radar? It might seem that radar must be free of the shortcomings of human observers, but again no. Clear skies can produce radar echoes by similar processes to those which cause visual mirages. A radar operator has the same problem as a visual observer. How can he tell if a blip on his

The most 'definite' of flying saucers (above) photographed in Brazil, turned out to be just a spectacular lenticular cloud formation.

screen is an insect, a bird, an atmospheric effect – or an extraterrestrial spacecraft? With so many sources of error, it is not surprising that radar UFOs are reported.

To illustrate the mistakes that can be made, in World War II a cruiser in the Mediterranean opened fire on and reported sinking a radar target that turned out to be a false image of the island of Malta. More tragically, during the Vietnam war in 1968 ground artillery and fighter aircraft were directed to attack a group of unidentified radar targets, presumed to be enemy helicopters launching an attack. The targets turned out to be spurious but an American patrol boat was accidentally sunk by the barrage and a destroyer was damaged. So radar – and radar operators – do make mistakes, and sometimes big ones.

The most provocative cases in the UFO literature are those claiming meetings with real aliens of the snow-on-their-boots variety. The originator of such stories was George Adamski, a former hamburger cook turned cult leader who in 1953 claimed to have met Venusians, Martians, and Saturnians, including 'two incredibly lovely young women'. And he also boasted of riding in their saucers to see cities, lakes, and woodlands on the far side of the Moon. Unfortunately, Adamski had not figured on the rapid advance of space technology which soon showed a rather different picture of our neighbour worlds.

Without doubt the most celebrated UFO encounter of all was the so-called interrupted journey of an American couple, Betty and Barney Hill. While driving home one evening in 1961 through the White Mountains of New Hampshire they spotted a UFO that seemed to be following their car – on the face of it not an exceptional sighting, and readily explained by the misidentification of a celestial object, in this case Jupiter (remember the Ohio police 'chase' of Venus). But what made the story exceptional was what happened subsequently.

A week after the sighting Mrs Hill began to have recurrent dreams that she and Barney had been abducted by aliens. UFO investigators managed to convince Mrs Hill that her dreams might be real, and that the couple had indeed been taken aboard a spaceship. The couple were examined under hypnosis by a psychiatrist, and it was during these hypnosis sessions that Betty Hill told a remarkable story about being medically examined by aliens aboard their spaceship.

UFOlogists naturally assumed that the testimony under hypnosis must prove the case. But that is not so. The psychiatrist concluded that Betty was simply retelling her dreams under hypnosis and that the abduction did not take place. Here we have not a hoax, but pure fantasy.

Needless to say, UFOlogists usually ignore the psychiatrist's professional opinion. But they cannot get away from the fact that there is no corroborating evidence; we have only the word of the Hills. Barney died some years ago, but Betty Hill has become deeply immersed in UFOlogy. She recently claimed to have discovered a UFO landing site. A UFO investigator who accompanied her there one night said afterwards: 'She is seeing things that are not UFOs and is calling them UFOs.' On one occasion she was reportedly unable to distinguish between a landed UFO and a street light.

Lack of independent corroboration bedevils all such abduction cases; the UFOs are totally successful at revealing themselves only to isolated humans. Hypnosis of the witness is not a truth test; it simply releases the same human fantasies that inspire such cases.

Two weeks after a TV programme about the Hill case was screened in 1975, an American forestry worker named Travis Walton claimed to have been taken aboard an alien spacecraft in northern Arizona for five days. He said that aboard the saucer he had met small creatures with domelike heads. Inevitably, it was too good a story to be left to the UFOlogists. Journalists from the sensational American newspaper the National Enquirer descended to interview Walton. One of those journalists, Jeff Wells, who has since left the paper, subsequently revealed the untold story behind the Walton case.

Among the characters involved was a celebrated UFOlogist, a California professor of engineering flown in specially by the newspaper, who was quick to comfort Walton: 'There are many people who have been chosen to meet them,' he said. ('I began to wonder about the professor,' recalls Wells.) Walton's brother was so encouraged he began to talk about his own UFO encounter as a child.

Unfortunately, when Walton was subjected to a lie-detector test he failed miserably. The examiner called it the plainest case of lying he had seen in 20 years, reports Wells. The local sheriff had claimed all along that the abduction was a hoax, as had the local UFO group who were first on the scene. Wells agreed and sat down to write a memo to his editors designed to kill the story. Imagine his surprise when, some weeks later, he found that his editors, with the help of the professor, had turned his memo into a front-page story. A panel of UFOlogists subsequently voted the Walton incident the top UFO case of 1975, and it is still widely championed in UFO books. Not surprisingly, credulous acceptance by UFOlogists of such abduction tales has inspired numerous imitators.

It is a favourite cry of UFOlogists that there is some great government conspiracy to prevent them – and us – from getting at the truth about UFOs. They admit that they do not have the evidence to prove their case, but instead argue that the government must have it but is covering it up. (This begs a rather

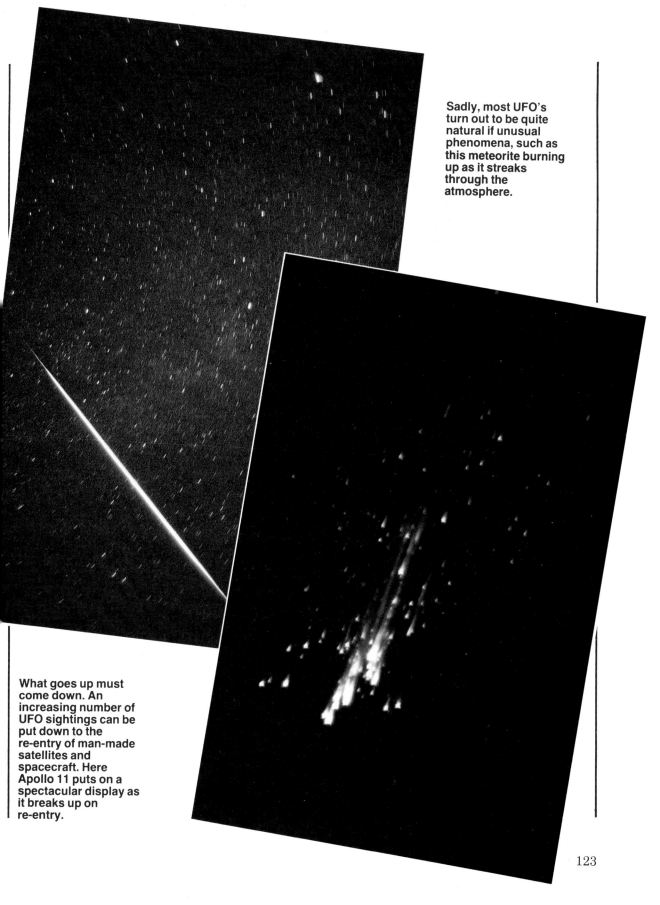

Sadly, most UFO's turn out to be quite natural if unusual phenomena, such as this meteorite burning up as it streaks through the atmosphere.

What goes up must come down. An increasing number of UFO sightings can be put down to the re-entry of man-made satellites and spacecraft. Here Apollo 11 puts on a spectacular display as it breaks up on re-entry.

123

obvious question). The ranks of UFO books which infest bookshops belie the existence of any cover-up. It seems strange in any case that anyone could believe that a UFO cover-up could be successfully operated by a succession of half a dozen United States Presidents, not to mention heads of other countries.

Unfortunately for the cover-up theory, the files of Project Blue Book, the former Air Force UFO office, have now been released and show that the Air Force knew no more about UFOs than anyone else – indeed a good deal less. So UFOlogists now say that the CIA was carrying out a secret study which even the Air Force did not know about.

Recently one thousand pages of CIA documents relating to UFOs have been released, which UFOlogists initially hailed as proof of the Cosmic Watergate they had been alleging. But examination of the files shows that they consist not of electrifying transcripts of cross-examination of aliens in smoke-filled rooms or engineers' reports on crashed flying saucers but of newspaper cuttings, letters from UFOlogists, and bureaucratic memos, averaging one page per week.

And what do the memos say? One, from 1953, reports that they had collected very little material worth keeping. Another, two years later, recommended that the part-time UFO project then being operated be terminated and the files placed in dead storage. An internal memo from 1976 states that the government has no UFO investigation in operation, nor is there any UFO programme in the intelligence community. This hardly sounds like evidence for a massive cover-up.

There is an effect at work which I term the UFO Uncertainty Principle which states that one cannot have a UFO sighting which is both highly reliable and highly specific. By a reliable sighting I mean one with many independent witnesses who all agree on what they have seen; when these occur the object is usually something unspecific like a light in the sky and quickly becomes identified, like the Carter sighting, the Zond 4 re-entry, and advertising planes. By specific sightings I mean those that speak of silvery craft and humanoid occupants. But these, like the

Adamski, Hill, and Walton cases, are totally unreliable.

By contrast, when something unexpected but undeniably real occurs, there is no shortage of evidence. For instance, in August 1972 a large meteorite sped through the atmosphere, missing the Earth's surface by a mere 65 kilometres before streaking out into space again. Despite the fact that it occurred over one of the least populated parts of the United States it was seen by thousands, including a meteor expert, it was widely photographed, and it was also detected by a US Air Force satellite. Needless to say, such a wide range of confirming evidence never accompanies alleged sightings of alien spacecraft. If UFOlogists had real evidence they would not need to invent government cover-ups or to endorse phoney cases.

Again, in December 1968 I and many other amateur astronomers saw a brilliant fuzzy object in the sky where no celestial object was supposed to be. It turned out to be a fuel dump from the Apollo 8 spacecraft on its way to the Moon. If real alien spacecraft were whizzing around in orbit they would rapidly be spotted both by visual astronomers and by defence radars which are actually designed to look for spaceships – our own.

Let us imagine that the occupants of an alien base somewhere in the solar system – say, the asteroid belt – want to send a scouting party to Earth. How would they go about it? The most efficient way would be similar to the way we would send an expedition to Mars. A large mother ship sets out carrying smaller entry probes. Once they had got here, the mother ship would stand off in orbit around the Earth while the entry probes, either automatic or with crews, dropped down to make first-hand investigations of the Earth and its inhabitants. Even if the entry probes went unnoticed, the mother ship would be sure to be spotted. Our own Skylab space station appeared as bright as the brightest stars in the night sky, and the Space Shuttle will make a similarly impressive appearance on its many missions.

Of course, none of this proves that the Earth is not being visited by aliens in spaceships that can somehow avoid detection by normal means. What it does demonstrate is that there is no good evidence to claim that we have yet observed as much as one alien spaceship. And after 35 years of searching by thousands of dedicated UFO believers around the world, that is a remarkably poor dividend.

In conclusion, it seems to me that the truth about UFOs is quite simple: it is rooted in human misperception, human self-delusion, and the quite natural human tendency to delude others. In other words, UFOs are a terrestrial phenomenon, not an extraterrestrial one. By studying UFOs we will learn not about extraterrestrial life or interstellar travel, but about human nature.

There are those who will be profoundly dissatisfied with this conclusion. I do not agree with them. For if searches for extraterrestrial radio signals and alien spacecraft both fail, there is an even more exciting conclusion to be drawn. The conclusion is that there is only one high-tech civilization in the Galaxy, and we are it. Then the people of Earth will inherit the Galaxy. Placed against such an elevating prospect, the thought that the Galaxy is already saturated with aliens seems less appealing.

Look hard at the stars, for they may yet be the birthright of mankind.

The best loved alien of them all, E.T. If non-fictional extraterrestrials bring such delight, those who greet them will be well pleased.

Index

Picture Credits

We thank the following organizations for permission to reproduce their photographs.

Robert Dixon 107; Mary Evans Picture Library 82; Michael Freeman 68, 75; Grumman Corporation 65; Robin Kerrod 91, 123; Maureen Lambray, John Hillelson Agency 125; NASA 12, 13, 19, 22, 25, 27, 29, 34, 38, 39, 41, 56, 57, 59, 63, 73, 83, 85, 87, 91, 113; National Astronomy and Ionosphere Center 109; National Film Archive 76; National Museum of Canada 103; Novosti 11, 12, 14, 42; Pekka Parviainen, British Astronomical Association 123 (top); Paul Popper Ltd 118, 119, 121; Tom Reiland, Allegheny Observatory 95; United States Naval Observatory 111

Artwork by Tudor Art Studios and Gillian Burgess